BASIC PROGRAMMING:
SELF-TAUGHT

BASIC PROGRAMMING: SELF-TAUGHT

Seymour C. Hirsch

Reston Publishing Company, Inc.
A Prentice-Hall Company
Reston, Virginia

Library of Congress Cataloging in Publication Data

Hirsch, Seymour C
    BASIC programming : self-taught.

    Includes index.
    1. Basic (Computer program language) I. Title.
QA76.73.B3H58   1980   001.6'424   79-13349
ISBN 0-8359-0432-6

© 1980 by
RESTON PUBLISHING COMPANY, INC.
A Prentice-Hall Company
Reston, Virginia 22090

10 9 8 7 6 5 4

Printed in the United States of America

TO ROBERTA

CONTENTS

PREFACE

This book was developed for those people who want to teach themselves BASIC in a relatively short time. Without attending a formal course, the reader should be able to acquire a sound working knowledge of all the major features of the BASIC programming language.

This book can also be used as the main text in a one- or two-semester course in computer programming. Despite the fact that the book is self-teaching, instructors can add the benefit of their own knowledge and experience. Instructors might want to assign additional problems of their own design.

The book teaches by example. Over 250 BASIC programs are reproduced. These programs, which were coded and machine tested especially for this book, illustrate BASIC's capabilities. In order to be simple and easy to understand, each program usually illustrates only one feature.

Nontechnical explanations are given in connection with the sample programs. These explanations cover points that might not readily be clear in the reproduced programs. The textual material was designed to provide pleasant, informal reading while, at the same time, providing the information required by the students. To get the most from the book, students should:

1. Read each chapter in its entirety quickly to get a general idea of what it covers.

2. Reread the chapter, making a special effort to understand most, if not all, of what it discusses.

3. Code the sample programs, run them, and then check the printouts to make sure that they essentially match those given in the text.

4. Experiment with the programs to see what happens when various statements are changed.

5. Answer the questions at the end of each chapter and machine test the assigned problems.

I would like to thank the many persons who helped with the development of this text, especially David Skalski, Guido Migiano, Diane Anderson, and my brother, Dr. Martin Hirsch.

Seymour C. Hirsch

INTRODUCTION

You can learn BASIC programming in just a few hours of study. This book guides you step by step with hundreds of examples from actual printouts. Study each example carefully and read the accompanying text. If you have a terminal at your disposal, try to reproduce each example and you will learn BASIC even faster. All set? Let's begin.

First, dial the computer system that you are authorized to use. Then respond to the system's questions. Logging on procedures differ from system to system, but here is an example of how one system operates. (The computer system types everything shown below except the underlined responses. You type those.)

```
TSS    11/10/78    1430

ID--DS1839

SYSTEM--BASIC

OLD OR NEW--NEW

NEW FILE NAME--TEST

READY
```

The computer system identified itself and then asked for your user ID. After receiving it, the system asked what programming language you wished to use. You replied BASIC. Then it asked whether you wanted to enter a brand new program or retrieve an old one. You responded NEW. The system requested a name for the new program, which you gave. Finally, the system typed READY. Note the name that you gave for the new program. Program names may consist of up to six characters made up of digits and letters of the alphabet.

You might now want to ask the computer to multiply 25 times 86 and print the result. Here is how you could accomplish the task.

```
10 PRINT 25*86
20 END

*RUN


        2150
```

You typed three lines. With the first line, you told the computer system to compute 25 times 86 and print the result (* means multiply). Then you told the system that there were no more instructions in the program. Finally, you requested the computer to *run* your program; that is, execute it to give the answer. The computer gave the answer. In this example, the answer is 2150.

The instructions you type ahead of RUN are called statements. Statements lead off with line numbers. The complete set of statements you enter to solve a problem is called a *program*. The *very last* statement of every program must be END.

The above program could have been written this way:

```
1 PRINT 25 * 86
2 END

*RUN


        2150
```

Note that the line numbers have been changed.

There are still other ways of writing the program. This way:

```
10 PRINT 25 * 86
35 END

*RUN


        2150
```

or this:

```
90000 PRINT 25 ✦ 86
99999 END

✦RUN

        2150
```

or many other ways.

    Line numbers may be as small as 1 or as large as 99999. They must be in increasing sequence. It is a good idea to put gaps between line numbers. (You might want to insert additional statements in your program later.)

    RUN is not a program statement. It is called a *system command.* It tells the computer system to run a program once you have entered all of it. In this text, *RUN and RUN are used interchangeably. Your system may not accept *RUN. In that case, use RUN wherever the illustrations in this text show *RUN. Spacing within statements is not important when you write a BASIC program. The above program could have been written this way:

```
10PRINT25✦86
20END

✦RUN

        2150
```

or this:

```
10 P R I N T 2 5 ✦ 8 6
20 E N D

✦RUN

        2150
```

or this:

```
10 PR IN T2 5✦8 6
20    EN    D

✦RUN

        2150
```

or many other ways.

Do not enter any more programs until additional information is given about how to do this at the end of this chapter. (Your program might go into a "loop" and cause a great deal of expense to your department.)

It is not recommended that you employ poor spacing techniques when you write a program. Try to imitate the examples in this book.

When you want the computer to make calculations, you may use the symbols + (add), - (subtract), * (multiply), / (divide), and ↑ (exponentiate). *Note:* All illustrative printouts in this text were computer-tested. The terminal that was used printed ^ whenever a ↑ was needed. Do not let this symbol concern you. In all the printouts within this book, the symbol ^ actually represents ↑.

Suppose you want the system to perform these calculations:

$$122 + 67 =$$
$$35 - 48 =$$
$$924 \times 83 =$$
$$\frac{17}{3.9} =$$
$$12.6^{3.1} =$$

You can write a program like this:

```
010 PRINT 122 + 67
020 PRINT 35 - 48
030 PRINT 924 * 83
040 PRINT 17 / 3.9
050 PRINT 12.6 ^ 3.1
060 END


*RUN


        189
        -13
      76692
    4.358974
    2577.203
```

A statement may contain several arithmetic operations. Example:

```
010 PRINT 26 * 85 * 35
020 PRINT 72 / 21 / 81
030 PRINT 24 * 23 / 71 / 33
040 END

*RUN

        77350
        .042328
        .2355954
```

The computer multiplies 26 by 85 and then multiplies the result by 35 and prints the answer. Next, the computer divides 72 by 21 and then divides the result by 81 and prints the answer. Then, the computer multiplies 24 by 23, divides the result by 71, and then divides that result by 33. Finally, the answer is printed.

If a statement includes additions and subtractions as well as multiplications and divisions, the computer system performs the multiplications and divisions before it does the additions and subtractions. Example:

```
10 PRINT 1.6 + 9.1 * 3.6 + 8 - 4.4
20 END

*RUN

        37.96
```

The computer multiplies 9.1 by 3.6, and then adds the result to 1.6. Next, it adds 8 and subtracts 4.4. Finally, the result is printed.

Another example:

```
10 PRINT 6.3 / 2.1 / 1.4 * 2.6 + 9.1 * 7.4
20 END

*RUN

        72.91143
```

The computer obtains two partial results. They are 6.3 divided by 2.1, the result divided by 1.4 and that result multiplied by 2.6; and 9.1 multiplied by 7.4. The two partial results are summed and printed.

If a statement includes exponentiations, they are performed ahead of multiplications and divisions and ahead of additions and subtractions. Example:

```
10 PRINT 6.8 ◆ 2.1 + 1.2 ^ 3 + 9.4 ⁄ 8.3 + 9.3 ^ 1.5
20 END

◆RUN

   45.50172
```

The computer system computes 1.2^3 and saves the result. It then computes $9.3^{1.5}$ and saves the result. Next, it multiplies 6.8 by 2.1 and 9.4 divided by 8.3 saving both results. The final action is to sum the four results and print the answer.

You may not like the computer's natural order of making computations. If so, place parentheses around quantities that are to be evaluated as units. Consider these examples:

$$\frac{9.5 + 1.7}{7.8 - 9.2} + 8.5 =$$

The program is written this way:

```
10 PRINT (9.5 + 1.7) ⁄ (7.8 - 9.2) + 8.5
20 END

◆RUN

    .5000003
```

Another example is:

$$\frac{4.8 - 7.6^{1.5}}{2.7} \times \frac{8}{5.1 + 7.3} =$$

which would be written:

```
10 PRINT ((4.8 - 7.6 ^ 1.5) ⁄ 2.7) ◆ (8⁄(5.1 + 7.3))
20 END

◆RUN

   -3.859439
```

It's all right to place extra parentheses in programs. Sometimes you are not sure what the program will do unless you put sufficient parentheses to ensure the results you need. Example:

$$\frac{\dfrac{1.3}{2.7 + 8.1}}{1.7 + 1.9} =$$

```
010 PRINT (1.3 / (2.7 + 8.1)) / (1.7 + 1.9)
020 END

◆RUN

    .0334362
```

The same results could be obtained this way:

```
10 PRINT 1.3 / (2.7 + 8.1) / (1.7 + 1.9)
20 END

◆RUN

    .0334362
```

If you're not sure whether or not it's necessary to do so, include extra parentheses. It's better to be safe than sorry.

You should now try all the examples that we have presented thus far. Before each program, type the system command NEW so that the system will not confuse one program with another. See the examples that follow.

```
TSS   11/10/78  1430
ID--DS1839
SYSTEM--BASIC
OLD OR NEW--NEW
NEW FILE NAME--TEST
READY
10 PRINT 25 ◆ 86
20 END
RUN

    2150
```

```
NEW
NEW FILE NAME--CALC
READY
10 PRINT 122 + 67
20 PRINT 35 - 48
30 PRINT 924 * 83
40 PRINT 17 / 3.9
50 PRINT 12.6 ^ 3.1
60 END
RUN
        189
        -13
      76692
    4.358974
    2577.203


NEW
NEW FILE NAME--ABC
READY
10 PRINT 26 * 85 * 35
20 PRINT 72 / 21 / 81
30 PRINT 24 * 23 / 71 / 33
40 END
RUN
      77350
     .042328
    .2355954
```

At the completion of a session with the computer, you disconnect by typing BYE. The system gives a sign-off message. Example:

```
BYE
TSS    11/10/78    1501
DISCONNECT    COST $2.30
THANK YOU
```

Now you take it from here.

EXERCISES

1. In your own words tell what this program does.

```
100 PRINT 25 * 86
110 END
RUN
```

2. Is RUN a program statement or is it a system command?

3. What are the five symbols that BASIC uses that cause calculations to take place? Give the meaning of each symbol.

4. Why are parentheses used when certain computations are made?

5. What is the rule about giving extra parentheses in a BASIC expression?

6. True or false? The following two BASIC statements always give the same results:

    A = (B + C)/(P - Q)
    A = B + C / P - Q

7. True or false? The following two BASIC statements always give the same results:

    F = (G / H)/N
    F = G / (H / N)

8. The programmer wishes to enter

    R = (T + V) / W

    However, he or she is a poor typist and actually enters

    R=(T+ V)/ W

    Will the statement be accepted correctly?

9. What are the smallest and largest line numbers permitted in BASIC?

10. What is the difference between a program statement and a system command?

11. Write a BASIC program that causes this calculation to take place:

    47 + 85 - 74.8 =

12. Write a BASIC program that causes this calculation to take place:

    347 X 92.6 X 75 =

13. Write a BASIC program that causes this calculation to take place.

$$\frac{84.5}{7.3} \times \frac{7.43}{1.2} =$$

14. Write a BASIC program that causes this calculation to take place:

$$\frac{\dfrac{7.5 + 9.7}{8}}{\dfrac{2.5}{1.7 - 5.8}} \times \frac{9.6}{1.5 - 2.8} =$$

15. Write a program that makes these calculations:

$$\frac{\dfrac{2.5}{8.3}}{9.6} =$$

$$\frac{2.5}{\dfrac{8.3}{9.6}} =$$

Why do the results differ even though the numbers are the same?

16. Write a program that makes these calculations:

$$(-2) \uparrow 4 =$$
$$-2 \uparrow 4 =$$

Why do the results differ even though the numbers are the same?

SYSTEM COMMANDS AND HOW TO MAKE CHANGES

When entering programs, you may type the statements of the programs in any sequence. The computer will sort the statements by line numbers in increasing sequence. Suppose, for example, you have written this program on a sheet of paper and intend to type it into the system like this:

```
010 LET F = 9.2
020 LET G = 4.5
030 LET H = F ◆ G
040 IF H>35 THEN 70
050 PRINT H
060 GO TO 80
070 PRINT F,G
080 END
```

Suppose that, when you type the program, you make two mistakes, entering it this way:

```
010 LET F = 9.2
020 LET G = 4.5
040 IF H>35 THEN 70
050 PRINT H
070 PRINT F,G
080 END
030 LET H = F ◆ G
060 GO TO 80
```

There is no problem; the program has been entered in the same sequence that it was written on your paper. You can prove this to yourself by asking the computer system to give you an up-to-date listing of your program. Simply type:

LIST

The system will give this printout:

```
010 LET F = 9.2
020 LET G = 4.5
030 LET H = F * G
040 IF H>35 THEN 70
050 PRINT H
060 GO TO 80
070 PRINT F,G
080 END
```

The system has sequenced the lines by their line numbers. This is a convenience to you since it allows you to insert statements in their proper places when entering your program should you inadvertently omit some.

When typing a statement, you might make a mistake before you return the carriage. If so, the character ← will enable you to correct the mistake. Example:

300 LET F = G +←* H

The user had intended to type

300 LET F = G * H

but typed a plus instead of an asterisk. The backwards arrow (←) backspaced the line *internally* and permitted the correction to be made. If more than one mistake is made, then more than one backspace symbol may be given. In the next example, the user intended to type:

10 LET R = (A + B) / (C - D)

The statement was actually entered this way:

10 LET R = (A + X) /←←←B) / (C - D)

Once an incorrect line has actually been entered, it must be retyped in order to change it. Suppose, for example, that a user had typed these lines:

```
10 LET J=6
20 LET N=4
30 PRIMP J*N
40 LET Q=7
50 LET R=3
60 PRINT J*N
70 PRINT Q*R
80 END
30 PRINT J*N
```

Note that line 30 has been retyped. The LIST command gives this output:

```
10 LET J=6
20 LET N=4
30 PRINT J*N
40 LET Q=7
50 LET R=3
60 PRINT J*N
70 PRINT Q*R
80 END
```

Statement 30, which had initially been entered incorrectly, now appears in correct form and in the correct place. A request to RUN gives this output:

```
*RUN

24
24
21
```

LIST and RUN are system commands.

If a statement is to be inserted into a program, you should select any desired line number between two existing line numbers and type the statement. For example, suppose you enter this program and run it:

```
10 LET X = 4
20 LET Y = 8
30 LET Z = X + Y
40 PRINT Z
50 END

◆RUN


          12
```

But you realize you should have added 9 at line 30. One way to make the change is this:

```
23 LET F = 9
30 LET Z = X + Y + F
RUN

       21
```

Line 23 was inserted between lines 20 and 30, and line 30 was changed to reflect the addition of 9.

To obtain a clean listing of your program type:

```
◆LIST

10 LET X = 4
20 LET Y = 8
23 LET F = 9
30 LET Z = X + Y + F
40 PRINT Z
50 END
```

It is not necessary to list a program before you run it, or vice versa. The RUN command could have been given instead of LIST.

To delete a statement from a program, type the line number only; then immediately return the carriage. Consider this example:

```
10 LET J = 9
20 LET K = 17
30 LET L = 3
40 PRINT J ◆ L
50 END

◆RUN


                27
```

It can be seen that there is no reason for line 20's presence, so delete the statement by typing the line number only.

```
                20
```

Running the program again, we should get the same output as before. List the program first:

```
LIST

10 LET J = 9
30 LET L = 3
40 PRINT J ◆ L
50 END
```

Then run it:

```
                ◆RUN


                27
```

The computer system tells you when you've made one or more mistakes. On the following page is a program with several errors.

```
10 LOT P = 25
20 LET Q = 2.6.9
30 PRINT P ◆ Q
40 GO TO 90
50 GO TO 70
60 GO TO 50
70 END

◆RUN
10 LOT P = 25
       ^

STATEMENT ERROR
20 LET Q = 2.6.9
             ^

STATEMENT ERROR
NO LINE NUMBER  90
```

There are problems with lines 10 and 20. There's also a problem with line 40 because it directs the program to line 90. There is no line 90 in the program. The errors are easily corrected by re-typing lines 10, 20, and 40:

```
10 LET P = 25
20 LET Q = 2.69
40 GO TO 60
```

Now, a request for a listing gives this:

```
◆LIST

10 LET P = 25
20 LET Q = 2.69
30 PRINT P ◆ Q
40 GO TO 60
50 GO TO 70
60 GO TO 50
70 END

◆RUN


          67.25
```

Of course, all those GO TO's at the end of the program are un-needed. We included them to illustrate the kinds of errors that the computer system catches.

To save a program, one types the system command SAVE. Example:

```
010 LET T = 6
020 LET V = 18
030 LET N = T - V
040 PRINT T,V,N
050 END
SAVE
FILE CAL SAVED
```

The system saves the file with the name you gave it earlier. To recall a saved program, type OLD when the system inquires NEW or OLD. The system will ask for the program's name. A programmer may type OLD when he or she is ready to begin working on an old program and give the program's name as shown in one of the examples below.

Consider the example that follows. First, the programmer enters a program and then runs it. (The program's name is X.)

```
010 LET G = 3
020 LET R = 7
030 LET T = G / R
040 PRINT G,R,T
050 END

◆RUN
```

```
          3                7          .4285714
```

Then the person saves it:

```
SAVE
FILE X SAVED
```

The next day the user retrieves the program by typing:

```
OLD X
```

The system responds READY and the user requests a listing, as shown on the following page.

```
READY

LIST

010 LET G = 3
020 LET R = 7
030 LET T = G / R
040 PRINT G,R,T
050 END
```

When a person is ready to begin working on a new program, he or she types NEW. For example, a person may have been doing this:

```
10 LET X = 14
20 LET Y = X^3
30 PRINT X,Y
40 END

*RUN

              14              2744
```

and then types:

```
NEW
NEW FILE NAME? SUMX
```

The computer requested a name for the new program; the programmer responded SUMX.

Since the previous program was not saved, the user will not be able to retrieve it at a later time. One saves only those programs that he or she wishes to retrieve in the future.

Saved programs may be unsaved by typing:

```
PURGE
```

Example:

```
PURGE XAMPL
FILE XAMPL PURGED
```

The user typed PURGE XAMPL; the system typed FILE XAMPL

PURGED and XAMPL was unsaved from the programmer's permanent storage area.

The command CATALOG is used when you wish to see what files you have in *saved* status. Example:

```
CATALOG
CAL
INTEG
TEST
MOVAVG
X
```

The user typed CATALOG; the system typed the names of all the files that were saved in the user's permanent storage area.

In this chapter, you learned the uses of several additional system commands. To review the system commands that you now know, study this table.

Command	Use
RUN	Execute a program
SAVE	Save a program
PURGE	Unsave a program
LIST	List a program
BYE	Disconnect from the system
OLD	Retrieve an old program
NEW	Begin working on a new program
CATALOG	Obtain a listing of saved programs

EXERCISES

1. How does the computer internally sort the statements that you enter?

2. What character do you use when you wish to correct a character that you typed incorrectly? (Assume you have not yet returned the carriage.)

3. May you use more than one backwards arrow when correcting characters in a BASIC statement?

4. What does the LIST system command do?

5. What does the RUN system command do?

6. How do you correct a BASIC statement that was entered into a program incorrectly? (The carriage was returned.)

7. How do you delete a line in a BASIC program?

8. Which system command do you give first—RUN or LIST? Does it make a difference as far as final results are concerned?

9. What does the SAVE system command do?

10. Do you ever type a line number ahead of a system command?

11. What does the system command BYE do?

12. Which of these words is *not* a system command?

LIST	RESUBMIT
SAVE	CATALOG
RUN	OLD
PURGE	NEW

13. In your own words, tell what a system command accomplishes when you process BASIC data processing problems.

14. After you have entered a program and have requested a run, how does the computer tell you that you made one or more mistakes.

15. How do you insert a statement into a BASIC program?

16. Study the following program:

```
10 LET X = 6
20 LET Q = 7
30 LET Y = 3
40 PRINT X,Y,X+Y
50 END
```

Show how you would delete line 20 from the program.

17. Study the following program:

```
10 LET A = 9
20 LET B = 13
30 LET C = 7
40 END
```

Show how you would insert a line that reads

```
PRINT A*B+C.
```

18. Study the following program:

```
10 LET P = 6
20 LET Q = 4
30 LET R = 7
40 PRINT P*Q+R
50 END
```

Show how you would change line 40 to read

PRINT P+Q*R.

3

THE ASSIGNMENT
STATEMENT

If a value is to be used in more than one place in a program, that
value may be assigned to a name. Study the use of W in this next
example:

```
010 LET W = 5.67298 / 3.5
020 PRINT 9.8 * W
030 PRINT 2.7 + W
040 PRINT W ^ 2
050 END

*RUN

   15.88434
   4.320851
   2.627159
```

The program prints three lines. The output is the same as if
the program had been written this way:

```
010 PRINT 9.8 * (5.67298 / 3.5)
020 PRINT 2.7 + (5.67298 / 3.5)
030 PRINT (5.67298 / 3.5) ^ 2
040 END
```

The first program requires less writing because the name W has been given to the value (5.67298/3.5).

A LET statement is used to assign names to values. The LET statement has this form:

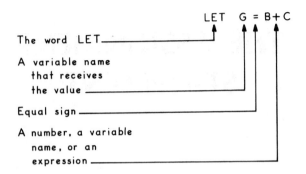

To name a value, give the value or expression on the right-hand side of an equal sign and the arbitrarily selected name on the lefthand side. The word LET begins the statement. Example:

```
010 LET A = 2.4
020 LET B = 9.2 / 3.3 + A
030 LET C = A + B
040 LET A = A + 1
050 PRINT A, B, C
060 END

◆RUN

        3.4        5.187879        7.587879
```

The program assigns 2.4 to A; then 9.2 / 3.3 + A (the same as 9.2 / 3.3 + 2.4) to B. Then the program sums A and B and names the result C. The calculation is 2.4 + (9.2 / 3.3 + 2.4). Finally the program increases the value of A by 1. This new value is 3.4. When A's value is updated, the previously computed values of B and C *remain unchanged*.

The names on the left of the equal signs are called *variable names* because their values can be changed as desired by a program. Those names may consist of single letters of the alphabet or single letters of the alphabet followed by single digits. These variable names are valid:

A

B

N

T3

D0

F5

These are not:

A33 (too long)

AX (a name can't consist of two letters of the alphabet)

3X (a name can't begin with a digit)

D* (a name can't include a special character such as *, +, #, etc.)

Another example:

```
010 LET R = 6.95
020 LET P = 3.1416
030 LET C = 2 * P * R
040 LET A = P * R ^ 2
050 LET V = (4/3) * P * R ^ 3
060 PRINT R, C, A, V
070 END
```

◆RUN

```
    6.95        43.66824        151.7471        1406.19
```

Note how values are assigned to R, P, C, A, and V.

The program could also have been written this way:

```
10 LET X1 = 6.95
20 LET X2 = 3.1416
30 LET X3 = 2 * X2 * X1
40 LET X4= X2 * X1 ^ 2
50 LET X5 = (4/3) * X2 * X1 ^ 3
60 PRINT X1, X3, X4, X5
70 END
```

◆RUN

```
  6.95        43.66824        151.7471        1406.19
```

The former program is preferred because the names R, P, C, A, and V stand for radius, pi, circumference, area, and volume. It's easy to associate those BASIC names with the values they stand for. It's more difficult to associate X1, X2, X3, X4, and X5 with radius, pi, circumference, area, and volume.

This next example shows that the program could be written using no assignment statements at all:

```
◆LIST

010 PRINT 6.95, 2◆3.1416◆6.95, 3.1416◆6.95^2, (4/3)◆3.1416◆6.95^3
020 END

◆RUN

        6.95         43.66824        151.7471         1406.19
```

EXERCISES

1. When would you give a name to a numeric value?
2. What is the special BASIC word that is used when it is required to give a name to a numeric value?
3. What does the statement LET A = 2.4 accomplish?
4. What does the statement LET B = 9.2/3.3 + A accomplish?
5. What does the statement LET A = A + 1 accomplish?
6. What is meant by the term *variable name*?
7. In BASIC, what are the rules for creating a variable name?
8. Study this program:

```
10 LET A = 5.6
20 LET B = 9.4
30 LET C = A * B
40 PRINT C
50 END
```

Rewrite the program so that it uses only two statements yet accomplishes the same task.

9. Tell what is wrong with these variable names:

    3X

    P–

    X33

    PD

10. Tell what actual values the following BASIC program will print:

        10 LET R = 48
        20 LET S = 12
        30 PRINT R/(S + 12)
        40 PRINT (R/S) + 12
        50 END

11. Write a program that computes

$$a = 3.5 + 9.3$$
$$b = 3.5 + 4.7$$
$$c = 9.3 + 4.7 + 8.7$$

    and prints the results. Give names to the values 3.5, 9.3, and 4.7.

12. Write a program that computes

$$3.8 + 4.9 - 7.6 =$$
$$1.4 - 6.6 + 5.8 =$$
$$3.7 \times 4.5 \times 7.6 =$$

    and prints the results. Do not give names to any of the values nor to the results. (Use the PRINT statement to compute the answers as well as print them.)

THE READ AND
DATA STATEMENTS

The numbers that a program uses can be placed in a DATA statement and then obtained with a READ statement. Example:

```
010 DATA 18, 44, 37, 91, 45
020 READ A
030 PRINT A
040 GO TO 20
050 END

◆RUN

          18
          44
          37
          91
          45

OUT OF DATA IN  20
```

The program obtains the value 18 from the DATA statement. That value is assigned to A. Then the program prints that value. The process is repeated. The next value, 44, is assigned to A and printed, and so on. Finally, the program runs out of values and prints the OUT OF DATA message.

29

When values are read, they can be used for computations. Example:

```
010 DATA 78, 32, 91, 56, 35
020 READ A
030 PRINT A, A^2
040 GO TO 20
050 END
```

◆RUN

```
        78              6084
        32              1024
        91              8281
        56              3136
        35              1225
```

OUT OF DATA IN 20

The program assigns 78 to A, then prints A and the square of A. Next the program assigns 32 to A and prints A and the square of A. Each new assignment to A replaces the previous value that A held.

A DATA statement may be located anywhere in a program as long as it is ahead of END. Example:

```
010 DATA 9, 2, 7, 4, 5
020 READ R
030 PRINT R, 2◆ 3.1416 ◆ R
040 GO TO 20
050 END
```

◆RUN

```
        9               56.5488
        2               12.5664
        7               43.9824
        4               25.1328
        5               31.416
```

OUT OF DATA IN 20

The program can also be written this way: (Note the location of the DATA statement.)

```
010 READ R
020 PRINT R, 2*3.1416 * R
030 GO TO 10
040 DATA 9,2,7,4,5
050 END


*RUN
```

```
        9           56.5488
        2           12.5664
        7           43.9824
        4           25.1328
        5           31.416

OUT OF DATA IN   10
```

The program runs the same as before.
     Another example where the data statement follows the READ statement:

```
010 READ R
020 DATA 9,2,7,4,5
030 PRINT R, 2*3.1416 * R
040 GO TO 10
050 END

*RUN
```

```
        9           56.5488
        2           12.5664
        7           43.9824
        4           25.1328
        5           31.416

OUT OF DATA IN   10
```

The program runs exactly the same as before.

It is a good idea to place all DATA statements at the head of the program or at the end just ahead of the END statement, like this:

```
010 READ H,R
020 PRINT H,R,H * R
030 GO TO 10
040 DATA 39.5, 5.50, 40.4, 4.80, 41.3, 5.60
050 DATA 38.7, 4.20, 37.6, 3.20
060 END

*RUN
```

39.5	5.5	217.25
40.4	4.8	193.92
41.3	5.6	231.28
38.7	4.2	162.54
37.6	3.2	120.32

```
OUT OF DATA IN   10
```

or this:

```
010 DATA 39.5, 5.50, 40.4, 4.80, 41.3, 5.60
020 DATA 38.7, 4.20, 37.6, 3.20
030 READ H,R
040 PRINT H,R,H * R
050 GO TO 30
060 END

*RUN
```

39.5	5.5	217.25
40.4	4.8	193.92
41.3	5.6	231.28
38.7	4.2	162.54
37.6	3.2	120.32

```
OUT OF DATA IN   30
```

Observe that values can be read two at a time, three at a time, or as many at a time as needed. There must be a *complete* set of values to be read; otherwise, the program gives the OUT OF DATA message. Example:

```
010 DATA 9.1, 6.3, 8.5, 9.8, 1.8
020 READ T,W
030 PRINT T,W,T / W
040 GO TO 20
050 END

♦RUN

        9.1              6.3          1.444444
        8.5              9.8          .8673469

OUT OF DATA IN  20
```

As you can see, the program prints two output lines. The program assigns 9.1 to T and 6.3 to W. Later it assigns 8.5 to T and 9.8 to W. The value 1.8 is not assigned to T since there is no companion value for W. (See the READ statement at line 20 which requires that values be read for *both* T and W.)

There may be as many DATA statements in a program as you need. Treat them as if they were one continuous DATA statement.

The READ statement has this form:

```
                              READ  X, Y, P
The word READ_____▲       ▲
A list of variable names_____|
```

The DATA statement has this form:

```
                         DATA     8, 2.6, 9, 7, 999
The word DATA _____▲          ▲
A list of data values_____|
```

EXERCISES

1. What does the READ statement accomplish in BASIC?
2. What does the DATA statement accomplish in BASIC?

3. In a BASIC program, where may the DATA statement be given?

4. How many DATA statements may you give in a BASIC program?

5. It is a good idea to place all DATA statements where?

6. How many values may a READ statement obtain from a DATA statement at a time?

7. When will a program give an OUT OF DATA message?

8. Study this next program:

```
10 DATA 8.2, 7.6, 4.1
20 READ A
30 PRINT A ↑ 2, A
40 GO TO 20
50 END
```

How many output lines will the program print?

9. Study this next program:

```
10 DATA 8,7,4,9,2,8,6,3
20 READ X,Y,Z
30 PRINT X*Y*Z
40 GO TO 20
50 END
```

How many output lines will the program print?

10. Refer to the program in Question 9. Add a data line just ahead of the END statement. That line is to hold only a single value. Rerun the program. How many output lines does the program print?

THE PRINT STATEMENT

The PRINT statement can be used for several purposes. First, it can be used to print the results of calculations defined within the PRINT statement itself. Example:

```
010 PRINT (4*6) / 1.5
020 PRINT 2.5 + 8.9, 7.5 * 8.4
030 PRINT .09 * 18.5
040 END

*RUN

          16
       11.4                63
        1.665
```

The PRINT statement can also be used to print values previously computed. Example:

```
010 LET A = 9.7
020 LET B = 4.9
030 LET C = A * B
040 LET D = A/B
050 LET E = (A + B) / 8.5
060 PRINT A,B,C,D,E
070 LET F = A^3
080 LET G = A^.5
090 PRINT A,B,F,G
100 END

*RUN

       9.7     4.9      47.53     1.979592     1.717647
       9.7     4.9     912.673    3.114482
```

As you can see, five values print across the page. Each area in which a value prints, is called a *zone*. Each zone has 15 print positions.

The PRINT statement can be used to print messages or remarks:

```
010 PRINT "THIS PROGRAM COMPUTES"
020 PRINT "THE SQUARE OF 5.8"
030 PRINT "IT ALSO PRINTS THE"
040 PRINT "CUBE OF 5.8."
050 PRINT 5.8^2, 5.8^3
060 PRINT "JOB COMPLETE."
070 END

◆RUN

THIS PROGRAM COMPUTES
THE SQUARE OF 5.8
IT ALSO PRINTS THE
CUBE OF 5.8.
          33.64            195.112
JOB COMPLETE.
```

Note that the program literally prints all messages that have been given within quotes. The quote marks, themselves, are not printed.

This next program gives a report having a report heading and column headings:

```
010 PRINT "THIS REPORT GIVES INVESTMENT YIELDS"
020 PRINT
030 PRINT "INVESTMENT","RATE","YIELD"
040 PRINT
050 PRINT 1500, .06, .06 ◆ 1500
060 PRINT 2750, .08, .08 ◆ 2750
070 PRINT 2000, .10, .10 ◆ 2000
080 PRINT
090 PRINT "END OF REPORT"
100 END

◆RUN

THIS REPORT GIVES INVESTMENT YIELDS

INVESTMENT      RATE               YIELD

          1500              .06               90
          2750              .08              220
          2000               .1              200

END OF REPORT
```

The "plain" PRINT statements at lines 20, 40, and 80 give blank lines. Note that when a PRINT statement gives a numeric value, that value is printed as given. Thus, the statement

> 70 PRINT 2000, .10, .10 * 2000

causes to be printed the actual values 2000, .10, and .10 × 2000. If the PRINT statement encloses the numeric values within quotes, a different output results. Example:

```
010 PRINT "THIS REPORT GIVES INVESTMENT YIELDS"
020 PRINT
030 PRINT "INVESTMENT", "RATE", "YIELD"
040 PRINT
050 PRINT "1500, .06, .06 * 1500"
060 PRINT "2750, .08, .08 * 2750"
070 PRINT "2000, .10, .10 * 2000"
080 PRINT
090 PRINT "END OF REPORT"
100 END

*RUN

THIS REPORT GIVES INVESTMENT YIELDS

INVESTMENT      RATE            YIELD

1500, .06, .06 * 1500
2750, .08, .08 * 2750
2000, .10, .10 * 2000

END OF REPORT
```

Admittedly, this is not a very useful printout. We give it here merely to show what happens when you ask the computer to print data enclosed within quotes.

Literal messages and numeric values can be included on the same print line. Example:

```
010 LET A = 2550
020 LET B = 36
030 LET C = 4570
040 PRINT "THE VALUE OF C IS";C
050 PRINT "THE VALUE OF B X C IS"; B * C
060 END

*RUN

THE VALUE OF C IS 4570
THE VALUE OF B X C IS  164520
```

Observe that the semicolons in the two PRINT statements cause
the message and the numeric values to be placed closer together.
Another example showing the use of semicolons is this:

```
010 LET A = 2.5
020 LET X = 19.6
030 LET Q = 21.6
040 LET Z = 48.694
050 LET D = 9.7
060 LET K = 45.6783
070 PRINT A, X, Q, Z, D, K
080 PRINT A; X; Q; Z; D; K
090 END
```

◆RUN

```
      2.5               19.6          21.6      48.694      9.7
      45.6783
2.5   19.6   21.6     48.694    9.7   45.6783
```

When commas are used, five values are printed per line. If
more than five values are requested, the computer system uses
another line. As we have seen, when semicolons are used, the
values are placed closer together. Of course, both commas and
semicolons may be used in a PRINT statement. Example:

```
010 LET A = 2.5
020 LET X = 19.6
030 LET Q = 21.6
040 LET Z = 48.694
050 LET D = 9.7
060 LET K = 45.6783
070 PRINT A, X; Q; Z, D; K
080 PRINT A; X; Q; Z, D, K
090 PRINT A; X, Q, Z; D, K
100 END
```

◆RUN

```
      2.5     19.6   21.6      48.694     9.7   45.6783
2.5   19.6   21.6       48.694          9.7        45.6783
2.5           19.6        21.6     48.694          9.7          45.6783
```

Whenever a comma is given, the program advances to the next
zone on the output paper. The exact points where zones begin
vary from system to system. The output given by your computer
may not match precisely the printout shown above.

A program may mix various types of outputs on one line.
Example:

```
010 LET R = 9.78
020 LET E = 2.71828
030 LET P = 3.14159
040 PRINT P; "RAD"; E*P, R; E; P, 91.83; "91.83"
050 END

*RUN

  3.14159 RAD    8.539721    9.78 2.71828      3.14159      91.83 91.83
```

The PRINT statement has this form:

$$\text{PRINT} \quad \text{"X VAL = ", X, 216, R+S}$$

The word PRINT⎯⎯⎯⎯⎯⎯⎯↑

A quoted message, variable
name, numeric value, and/or an
expression (or none of these) ⎯⎯⎯⎯⎯↑

EXERCISES

1. List three ways that a PRINT statement can be used in a program.

2. Study this program:

   ```
   10 PRINT (36 + 8) / 11
   20 END
   ```

   What will the program print?

3. Study this program:

   ```
   10 PRINT "THIS IS A SAMPLE MESSAGE"
   20 END
   ```

   What will the program print?

4. Study this program:

   ```
   10 LET X = 5
   20 LET Y = 6
   30 LET Z = X * Y
   ```

```
40  LET Y = 9
50  PRINT X, Y, Z
60  END
```

What will the program print?

5. Study this program:

```
10  PRINT "X", "Y", "Z"
20  END
```

What will the program print? Approximately how many unused print positions will there be between X and Y, and between Y and Z?

6. When variable names in a PRINT statement are separated by
commas, how many lines will the computer need in order to
execute the following PRINT statement?

```
10  LET R = 6.3
20  LET T = 9.4
30  LET U = 6.2
40  LET W = 8.6
50  LET Z = 5.5
60  PRINT R, T, U, W, Z
70  END
```

7. What does the statement

```
40  PRINT
```

accomplish in a program?

8. Study this program:

```
10  LET G = 7.7
20  PRINT "THE VALUE OF G IS";G
```

What will the program print?

9. Explain the difference between

```
40  PRINT R, F, H, N, T
```

and

```
50 PRINT R; F; H; N; T
```

10. Study the statement that follows:

```
60 PRINT A, B; C; D; E, F
```

Will BASIC accept this statement?

11. Run this program.

```
10 LET A = 4.56
20 LET B = 2.91
30 LET C = 7.84
40 PRINT A; B; C, A+B, "*"
50 END
```

In what print position does the asterisk print?

12. Run this program:

```
10 LET P = 4.8
20 LET Q = 8.7
30 LET R = 1.4
40 PRINT P; Q; R; 4.8; 8.7; 1.4; "*"
50 END
```

In what print position does the asterisk print?

13. Write a program that prints 20 asterisks beginning at column 10 of the output paper.

14. Write a program that prints this design (ampersand):

CALCULATIONS

In BASIC, calculations may be done with the aid of the arithmetic operators +, -, /, *, and ↑. Let's consider addition (+) and subtraction (-) first.

```
010 LET X=3
020 LET Y=5
030 LET A=X+Y
040 LET B=X-Y
050 PRINT X,Y,A,B
060 END

◆RUN
```

```
        3           5           8          -2
```

The values of X and Y are summed; the result is assigned to A. Next, the value of Y is subtracted from X; the result is assigned to B. The values of X, Y, A, and B are then printed.

In the example on the following page, we will see how other values can be combined with plus and minus signs.

```
10 LET X=3
20 LET Y=5
30 LET Z=9
40 LET A=X+Y
50 LET B=X-Y
60 LET C=Y+X
70 LET D=-X-6+Y-Z
80 LET E=24-X-Y-Z
90 PRINT X;Y;Z;A;B;C;D;E
100 END

◆RUN

     3     5     9     8    -2     8   -13     7
```

The next example shows that, after Z's value is changed, any further calculations involving Z use the *last* value assigned to Z.

```
10 LET X=3
20 LET Y=5
30 LET Z=2
40 LET A=X+Y-Z
50 LET Z=8
60 LET B=X+Y-Z
70 LET C=3-X-Y-Z
80 PRINT X;Y;Z;A;B;C
90 END

◆RUN

     3     5     8     6     0   -13
```

To multiply, the asterisk is used:

```
10 LET X=4
20 LET Y=2
30 LET Z=8
40 LET A=X◆Y
50 LET B=Y◆Z
60 LET C=X◆Y◆Z◆3
70 PRINT X;Y;Z;A;B;C
80 END

◆RUN

     4     2     8     8    16   192
```

The value of X is multiplied by the value of Y. The result is assigned to A. Later, the value is printed. Similarly, Y is multiplied by Z and, later, the result is printed. The value for C is computed by multiplying X by Y by Z by 3.

To indicate divisions, the slash is used. In the next example, X is divided by Y, and the result is assigned to A. Later, that result is printed. A different answer is given when Y is divided by X. The result is assigned to B. Finally, X is divided by Y, the *result* is divided by Z, and *that result* is divided by 3. The final answer is assigned to C.

```
10 LET X=4
20 LET Y=2
30 LET Z=9
40 LET A=X/Y
50 LET B=Y/X
60 LET C=X/Y/Z/3
70 PRINT X;Y;Z;A;B;C
80 END

◆RUN

    4     2     9     2    .5    .0740741
```

Another example in division follows. Study the results to make sure you understand how they were computed.

```
10 LET X=4
20 LET Y=7
30 LET Z=8
40 LET A=X/Y
50 LET B=Z/A
60 LET C=B/A
70 PRINT X;Y;Z;A;B;C
80 END

◆RUN

    4     7     8    .5714286    14   24.5
```

When multiplications and divisions are given in the same expression, evaluations take place from left to right. In the first calculation below, X is multiplied by Y, and the *result* is divided by Z. In the second calculation, Y is divided by X, and the *result* is multiplied by Z. In the third calculation, Z is multiplied by X, the *result* is divided by Z, and *that result* is divided by 4.

```
10 LET X=6
20 LET Y=8
30 LET Z=2
40 LET A=X*Y/Z
50 LET B=Y/X*Z
60 LET C=Z*X/Z/4
70 PRINT X;Y;Z;A;B;C
80 END
```

◆RUN

```
 6     8     2     24     2.666667    1.5
```

Values can be raised to powers using the operation symbols ↑ and/or **. Thus, in the next example, X is raised to the Y power, Z is raised to the fourth power, and, finally, Z is raised to the fourth power in another way. The results are shown below.

```
10 LET X=5
20 LET Y=6
30 LET Z=2
40 LET A=X^Y
50 LET B=Z^4
60 LET C=Z**4
70 PRINT X;Y;Z;A;B;C
80 END
```

◆RUN

```
 5     6     2     15625     16     16
```

Two arithmetic operators may not be placed next to each other. In the example below, "060 LET C = Z ↑ -5" is not allowed because the minus sign is placed next to the exponentiation symbol. Note that the computer gives an error message when an attempt is made to run the program.

```
010 LET X=5
020 LET Y=6
030 LET Z=2
040 LET A=X^4.2
050 LET B=Y^7.8
060 LET C=Z^-5
070 PRINT X;Y;X;A;B;C
080 END


◆RUN
060 LET C=Z^-5
            ^
STATEMENT ERROR
```

The problem is resolved by placing −5 in parentheses, like this:

```
010 LET X=5
020 LET Y=6
030 LET Z=2
040 LET A=X^4.2
050 LET B=Y^7.8
060 LET C=Z^(-5)
070 PRINT X;Y;Z;A;B;C
080 END

◆RUN


  5     6     2   862.331  1173761    .03125
```

When the + and * symbols are given in the same expression, multiplications are performed ahead of additions. In the examples that follow, the calculations performed are:

$$a = X + (Y * Z)$$

$$b = (X * Y) + Z$$

$$c = (X * T) + (Z * 3)$$

```
010 LET X=4
020 LET Y=9
030 LET Z=6
040 LET A=X+Y◆Z
050 LET B=X◆Y+Z
060 LET C=X◆Y+Z◆3
070 PRINT X;Y;Z;A;B;C
080 END

◆RUN
```

$$4 \quad 9 \quad 6 \quad 58 \quad 42 \quad 54$$

Divisions are also performed ahead of additions. In the examples that follow, the calculations made are:

$$a = X + \frac{Y}{Z}$$

$$b = \frac{X}{Y} + Z$$

$$c = \frac{X}{Y} + \frac{Z}{3}$$

```
10 LET X=4
20 LET Y=9
30 LET Z=6
40 LET A=X+Y/Z
50 LET B=X/Y+Z
60 LET C=X/Y+Z/3
70 PRINT X;Y;Z;A;B;C
80 END

◆RUN
```

$$4 \quad 9 \quad 6 \quad 5.5 \quad 6.444444 \quad 2.444444$$

Exponentiations take precedence above multiplications, divisions, additions, and subtractions. In the following example, the calculations made are:

$$a = X^2 + Y^3 + Z^4$$
$$b = X^2 + (Y^3 * Z)$$
$$c = (X * Y^2) + (X * Y^3 * Z)$$

```
10 LET X=4
20 LET Y=9
30 LET Z=6
40 LET A=X^2+Y^3+Z^4
50 LET B=X^2+Y^3*Z
60 LET C=X*Y^2+X*Y^3*Z
70 PRINT X;Y;Z;A;B;C
80 END

*RUN

    4    9    6  2041  4390    17820
```

In expressions, when parentheses are not used, the order of operations is:

First—exponentiations

Second—multiplications and divisions in sequence as the expression is processed from left to right.

Third—additions and subtractions in sequence as the expression is processed from left to right.

This automatic sequence can be altered as desired by the use of parentheses. In this next example, the calculations made are:

$$a = \frac{X + Y}{Z}$$

$$b = \frac{X}{Y + Z}$$

and

$$c = \frac{\dfrac{X + 3}{Y - 4}}{Z + 4}$$

Note how parentheses ensure that the exact calculations desired are made in the program on the next page.

```
10 LET X=5
20 LET Y=7
30 LET Z=9
40 LET A=(X+Y)/Z
50 LET B=X/(Y+Z)
60 LET C=(X+3)/(Y-4)/(Z+4)
70 PRINT X;Y;Z;A;B;C
80 END
```

♦RUN

    5   7   9   1.333333   .3125   .2051282

At line 60, if this calculation had been desired

$$c = \frac{X + 3}{\dfrac{Y - 4}{Z + 4}}$$

the statement would have been written:

    60 LET C = (X + 3)/((Y - 4)/(Z + 4))

In the next example, the calculations made are:

$$a = \frac{\dfrac{X}{Y}}{Z}$$

$$b = \frac{\dfrac{X}{Y}}{Z}$$

and $$c = \frac{X}{\dfrac{Y}{Z}}$$

```
10 LET X=5
20 LET Y=7
30 LET Z=9
40 LET A=X/Y/Z
50 LET B=(X/Y)/Z
60 LET C=X/(Y/Z)
70 PRINT X;Y;Z;A;B;C
80 END
```

♦RUN

    5   7   9   .0793651   .0793651   6.428571

If you are not sure whether the built-in priority of operations will accomplish what you want, then parentheses should be placed in expressions. If necessary, parentheses within parentheses may be used. Do not fear giving too many parentheses; they will not hurt providing you correctly define what is needed. Study the following example:

```
10 LET X=5
20 LET Y=7
30 LET Z=9
40 LET A=(X+3)/(Y-4)/(Z+4)
50 LET B=((X+3)/(Y-4))/(Z+4)
60 LET C=(X+3)/((Y-4)/(Z+4))
70 PRINT X;Y;Z;A;B;C
80 END

◆RUN

   5      7      9    .2051282    .2051282    34.66667
```

The parentheses clearly define the quantities that are to be calculated.

Parentheses are sometimes critical where exponentiations are to be performed. In the next example, the calculations performed are:

$$a = -(X^3)$$
$$b = (-X)^3$$
and
$$c = (-Y)^z$$

```
10 LET X=3
20 LET Y=4
30 LET Z=5
40 LET A=-X^3
50 LET B=(-X)^3
60 LET C=(-Y)^Z
70 PRINT X;Y;Z;A;B;C
80 END

◆RUN

      3      4      5    -27    -27  -1024
```

The next two example programs give identical results. Study especially line 140 in the program that follows. A rather complex calculation is made in a single line.

```
010 LET A=2
020 LET B=3
030 LET C=5
040 LET D=8
050 LET E=10
060 LET F=12
070 LET G=4
080 LET H=6
090 LET J=9
100 LET K=11
110 LET L=15
120 LET M=16
130 LET N=20
140 LET P=A+(((B-C/D)^2*E*F)-G*(H^2*J-K)+L)/(M*N)
150 PRINT A;B;C;D;E;F;G
160 PRINT H;J;K;L;M;N;P
170 END

*RUN

    2      3      5      8     10     12      4
    6      9     11     15     16     20    .2496094
```

Then contrast the calculation with those shown on lines 140 through 200 in the next program. The same calculation as that made in line 140 of the preceding program is made in short steps. Note that the values of T7 and P are the same.

```
010 LET A=2
020 LET B=3
030 LET C=5
040 LET D=8
050 LET E=10
060 LET F=12
070 LET G=4
080 LET H=6
090 LET J=9
100 LET K=11
110 LET L=15
120 LET M=16
130 LET N=20
140 LET T1=B-(C/D)
150 LET T2=((H^2)*J)-K
160 LET T3=M*N
170 LET T4=(T1^2)*E*F
180 LET T5=T4-(G*T2)+L
190 LET T6=T5/T3
200 LET T7=A+T6
210 PRINT T7
220 LET P=A+(((B-C/D)^2*E*F)-G*(H^2*J-K)+L)/(M*N)
230 PRINT A;B;C;D;E;F;G
240 PRINT H;J;K;L;M;N;P
250 END
```

◆RUN

```
.2496094
2       3       5       8      10      12      4
6       9      11      15      16      20      .2496094
```

The next example shows how computed results can be printed under column headings.

```
010 PRINT "        NUM        NUM SQ′D        NUM CUBED"
020 PRINT
030 LET X=4
040 LET A=X^2
050 LET B=X^3
060 PRINT X,A,B
070 LET Y=5
080 LET C=Y^2
090 LET D=Y^3
100 PRINT Y,C,D
110 END
```

◆RUN

```
    NUM            NUM SQ′D        NUM CUBED

     4                16              64
     5                25             125
```

It requires a bit of careful planning to cause a heading to print precisely centered above the value it identifies.

Numeric values can be expressed as powers of 10. In the next example, 4.5E6 is seen to represent 4500000.

```
010 LET A=4.5E6
020 LET B=4500000
030 PRINT A,B
040 END
```

◆RUN

```
    4500000         4500000
```

The number that follows E is a power of 10. Thus, E6 means "times 10^6."

The next example shows that a selected number can be expressed in many ways.

```
010 LET A=4.5E3
020 LET B=.45E4
030 LET C=.045E5
040 LET D=45E2
050 LET E=45000E-1
060 PRINT A;B;C;D;E
070 END

◆RUN


    4500    4500    4500    4500    4500
```

You can use numbers expressed as powers of 10 (exponential notation) freely in a program. In the following program, 2.5E2 represents 250 and 1.5E-1 represents 0.15.

```
10 LET A=34.
20 LET B=5.6
30 LET C=2.5E2
40 LET D=(A+B)/C+1.5E-1
50 PRINT A;B;C;D
60 END

◆RUN


    34    5.6    250    .3084
```

The next example shows that any given power of 10 can be expressed many ways. Note the various ways that 10^4 is represented.

```
010 LET A=3.4E4
020 LET B=3.4E04
030 LET C=3.4 E 04
040 LET D=3.4E+04
050 LET E=3.4E 00004
060 PRINT A;B;C;D;E
070 END

◆RUN



    34000    34000    34000    34000    34000
```

Observe in the next example that the computer system some-times gives results in exponential notation:

```
◆010 LET A=.000003
◆020 LET B=34.99E25
◆030 LET C=45
◆040 LET D=(A+B)/C
◆050 PRINT A;B;C;D
◆060 END
◆070
◆RUN
```

```
3.00000E-06      3.49900E 26      45  7.77556E 24
```

The system selects what it considers the best or most accurate way to give you an answer.

The next program summarizes powers of 10. Note that 1×10^{-4} is $\frac{1}{10000}$, that 1×10^{-3} is $\frac{1}{1000}$, etc.

```
010 LET A=1E-4
020 LET B=1E-3
030 LET C=1E-2
040 LET D=1E-1
050 LET E=1E 0
060 LET F=1E 1
070 LET G=1E 2
080 LET H=1E 3
090 LET I=1E 4
100 PRINT A;B;C;D;E;F;G;H;I
110 PRINT "   ";-4;-3;" ";-2;-1;0;1;2;3;4
120 END
```

```
◆RUN
```

```
.0001  .001  .01   .1    1    10   100  1000   10000
  -4    -3   -2   -1    0    1    2    3      4
```

The program gives the table on the following page.

Exponent	Meaning	Example
E-4	$\dfrac{1}{10000}$	.45E-4 means .000045
E-3	$\dfrac{1}{1000}$	.45E-3 means .00045
E-2	$\dfrac{1}{100}$	.45E-2 means .0045
E-1	$\dfrac{1}{10}$	.45E-1 means .045
E 0	1	.45E0 means .45
E 1	10	.45E1 means 4.5
E 2	100	.45E2 means 45
E 3	1000	.45E3 means 450
E 4	10000	.45E4 means 4500

Many BASIC systems permit numbers to be expressed within the range $\pm 1 \times 10^{\pm 99}$. Thus, numbers like 4.5694×10^{60} or -8.29456×10^{-75} are well within the permissible range in BASIC.

EXERCISES

1. What five arithmetic operators may you use in order to have the computer perform calculations?

2. Study this program.

   ```
   10 LET D = 15 * 4
   20 PRINT 15, 4, D
   30 END
   ```

   What will the program print?

3. Study this program.

   ```
   10 PRINT 15, 4, 15 * 4
   20 END
   ```

   What will the program print? How is the program in Question 3 different from the program in Question 2?

4. Study this program:

```
10 LET A = 5
20 LET B = 8
30 LET C = A + B
40 PRINT A, B, C
50 END
```

What will the program print? Approximately how far apart will all values be on the printed line?

5. Study this program:

```
10 LET A = 5
20 LET B = 8
30 LET C = A * B
40 LET D = A / B
50 PRINT A, B, C, D
60 END
```

What will the program print?

6. Study this program:

```
10 LET A = 5
20 LET B = 8
30 LET C = 10
40 PRINT A * B / C
50 END
```

What will the program print?

7. Study this program:

```
10 PRINT 10 * 6 - 12 / 4
20 END
```

What will the program print?

8. What is wrong with this statement?

```
60 LET C = Z ↑ - 5
```

How should the statement be corrected?

9. Write the BASIC commands that cause the following computations to take place in a BASIC program:

$$6 + \frac{12}{88} =$$

$$\frac{15}{5} + 18 =$$

$$\frac{15}{3} + \frac{18}{3} =$$

10. In an arithmetic expression, which operation (exponentiation, addition, subtraction, multiplication, division) is performed first?

11. Why should you use parentheses in a BASIC expression?

12. Do the statements

```
100  LET X = Y / Z / R
110  LET X = Y / (Z / R)
120  LET X = (Y / Z) / R
```

cause the same value to be assigned to X?

13. Will more than enough parentheses harm your BASIC program in any way?

14. What value does the term 4.5E4 represent?

15. What value does the term .45E-1 represent?

16. Run this program:

```
10  LET A = (2.5 / 6.25) ↑ 2 + .50 * .50
20  PRINT A
30  END
```

Before the program runs, tell what you expect the answer to be.

17. Run a program that makes these calculations:

$$\frac{\dfrac{1.5E4}{3.9E5} \times \dfrac{8.9E2}{2.6E2}}{9.7E4} =$$

18. Run the same program as in Question 17 using ordinary numbers.

FUNCTIONS

BASIC makes available several built-in routines that accomplish desirable objectives. For example, you might want to obtain the square root of a number or the sine of an angle. In the example that follows, the square roots of 2, Y, and (X + Y) / Z are being computed. Also, the square root of a sum of square roots is being computed.

```
010 LET X=2
020 LET Y=5
030 LET Z=10
040 LET A=SQR(2)        square root
050 PRINT A
060 LET B=SQR(Y)
070 PRINT B
080 LET C=SQR((X+Y)/Z)
090 PRINT C
100 LET D=SQR(SQR(X)+SQR(Y)+SQR(Z))
110 PRINT D
120 END

◆RUN

     1.414214
     2.236068
      .83666
     2.610088
```

The name of the built-in function being used is SQR. The argument of the function—the value that the function is to work with—is placed within parentheses following the name of the function. Observe that an argument may be a number, for example, 2; a name, for example, Y; or an expression, for example, (X + Y)/Z. The argument must be positive; otherwise, the computer will give an error message.

In the next example, the sine of X, the cosine of Y, and the logarithm of Z are being computed.

```
010 LET X=2
020 LET Y=5
030 LET Z=10
040 LET A=SIN(X)
050 LET B=COS(Y)
060 LET C=LOG(Z)
070 PRINT A;B;C
080 END

◆RUN

 .9092974    .2836622    2.302585
```

In sine, cosine, and tangent functions (SIN, COS, TAN), arguments must be provided in radian measure. The logarithm function (LOG) computes natural logarithms (base "e").

The INT function obtains the integer portion of a number. The next example shows that the integer portion of 34.567 is 34, and the integer portion of 34.234 is also 34.

```
010 LET X=34.567
020 LET Y=34.234
030 LET A=INT(X)
040 LET B=INT(Y)
050 PRINT X;Y;A;B
060 END

◆RUN

 34.567   34.234    34    34
```

Where a number is negative, the integer portion of the number might be an unexpected, yet a mathematically correct, one. In the next example, the integer portion of -34.567 and also of -34.234 is seen to be -35.

```
010 LET X=-34.567
020 LET Y=-34.234
030 LET A=INT(X)
040 LET B=INT(Y)
050 PRINT X;Y;A;B
060 END

◆RUN

    -34.567   -34.234    -35    -35
```

The EXP function raises "e" to a given power. In the example that follows $e^{4.5}$ is seen to be 90.01713. The solution has been worked out two ways.

```
010 LET X=4.5
020 LET A=EXP(X)
030 LET B=2.718281828^X
040 PRINT X;A;B
050 END

◆RUN

   4.5     90.01713    90.01713
```

The ATN function gives the arctangent of a numeric argument. The angle is given in radian measure:

```
010 LET X=.5
020 LET A=ATN(X)
030 PRINT A
040 END

◆RUN


    .4636476
```

Another example can be seen on the next page.

```
010 LET X=34
020 LET A=ATN(X)
030 PRINT A
040 END

◆RUN


     1.541393
```

One may request a random number by using the RND function. The random number given falls within the range

$$0 \leqslant R < 1$$

where R is the random number given. The random number given by the computer lies between zero and one. Zero can actually appear as a random number, but 1 cannot. Example:

```
010 LET X=-1
020 LET A=RND(X)
030 PRINT A
040 END

◆RUN

     .7847689
```

Chapter 18 gives more information about random numbers and the RND function.

The ABS function gives the absolute value of a given argument. In the next example, the absolute values of 55 and –55 are seen to be 55. (The absolute value of a number is the positive form of that number.)

```
010 LET X=55
020 LET Y=-55
030 LET A=ABS(X)
040 LET B=ABS(Y)
050 PRINT X;Y;A;B
060 END

◆RUN

    55   -55   55   55
```

EXERCISES

1. What is a BASIC function?

2. What is the name of the BASIC function that computes square roots?

3. What are the names of the functions that compute sines, cosines, logarithms, and tangents?

4. What is the integer portion of the number 34.675?

5. What is the integer portion of the number 34.123?

6. What is the name of the BASIC function that computes integer values?

7. What does the BASIC function EXP do?

8. What does the function ATN do?

9. When BASIC is asked to deliver a random number, what is the range of numbers from which the random number is obtained?

10. What is the absolute value of the number −81.6?
    What is the absolute value of the number 81.6?
    What is the name of the function that gives absolute values?

11. What is the "argument" of a function?

12. What three forms may arguments take when used with functions?

13. Write a BASIC program that computes the square root of 25.

14. Write a BASIC program that gives the integer portion of the value −83.67.

15. Write a program that attempts to obtain the square root of −36. What does the computer do?

16. Write a program that obtains the absolute value of −38.745 and prints the result.

17. Show that the sine of an angle divided by the cosine of the same angle gives the tangent of the angle.

18. Show that raising a number to the $\frac{1}{2}$ power is a way of obtaining the square root of the number.

THE IF STATEMENT

A program can take alternate courses as it solves a problem. For example, assume you want to know whether 16% of $2000 is a better return on an investment than 14% of $2300. A program to determine the answer is:

```
010 LET X=.16 ◆ 2000
020 LET Y=.14 ◆ 2300
030 IF X>Y THEN 90
040 IF X=Y THEN 70
050 PRINT ".14 IS BETTER"
060 GO TO 100
070 PRINT "BOTH ARE EQUAL"
080 GO TO 100
090 PRINT ".16 IS BETTER"
100 END

◆RUN

.14 IS BETTER
```

In IF statements, the words "GO TO" may be used in place of "THEN." Be careful, though. Not all systems accept "GO TO." It might be better always to use "THEN." The IF statement permits conditions to be tested. If the result of the test is "true," the program takes the indicated jump. If the result is "false," the program goes to the next statement of the program. The IF statement has this form:

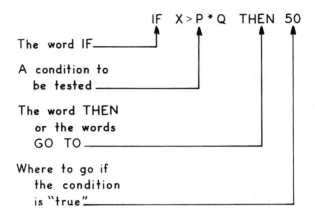

Values used in IF statements may be numbers, such as 83, 92, and −75; variable names, such as D, A5, and T; and BASIC expressions, such as A + B, (D + R) / T, and A + SIN(W).

Some ways to use IF statements are these:

        If A = B THEN 800
        IF P > 6.5 THEN 30
        IF J > = P − R THEN 300
        IF 16 < = (R + S) / T THEN 25
        IF A * B < T / V THEN 550
        IF R < > 7.2 THEN 890

The meanings of the symbols are these:

        =   equal
        >   greater than
        <   less than
        <>   not equal
        > =   greater than or equal
        < =   less than or equal

Suppose we need to sum some values given in a DATA statement. The sum can be computed this way:

```
010 DATA 8, 2, 9, 15, 3, 1000
020 LET S=0
030 READ X
040 IF X = 1000 GO TO 70
050 LET S=S+X
060 GO TO 30
070 PRINT S
080 END

◆RUN

    37
```

The program reads and sums values until the *dummy* value 1000 is detected. At that time, the program jumps to statement 70 where the value of S is printed.

A dummy value can be any value that the programmer knows with certainty will never conflict with an *actual* data value to be read into the program. The dummy value can be a very high number, a very low number, zero (sometimes), or any other value that makes sense to use. Here is an example where various values are being summed. Assume that it is known that no values are negative. The value −1 is a dummy. It signals the fact that all values in the DATA statement have been processed. The IF statement at line 040 tests whether the dummy has been read.

```
010 DATA 10, 16, 8, 9, 17, -1
020 LET S = 0
030 READ V
040 IF V<0 THEN 70
050 LET S=S+V
060 GO TO 30
070 PRINT S
080 END

◆RUN

    60
```

If this program is to be used many times, the only statement that needs to be changed each time the program is run is the DATA statement. For convenience, the dummy value can be placed on a line of its own. An example follows on the next page.

```
010 DATA 6, 9, 18, 14, 3, 15
020 DATA -1
030 LET S=0
040 READ V
050 IF V < 0 THEN 80
060 LET S = S+V
070 GO TO 40
080 PRINT S
090 END
```

◆RUN

65

Note that the dummy value, -1, is located by itself on line 020.

If you want an average of values in a DATA statement, the values must be counted as they are read and summed. Example:

```
010 DATA 19, 17, 10, 18, 21, 41, 14
020 DATA -1
030 LET S=0
040 LET C=0
050 READ V
060 IF V<0 THEN 100
070 LET S = S+V
080 LET C = C + 1
090 GO TO 50
100 PRINT S/C
110 END
```

◆RUN

20

The variable C is the counter in this program. Every time that V is added to S, 1 is added to C.

Suppose you need to know whether a series of numeric values are in numerically increasing sequence. Here is a program that makes the test. (The value 1000 in the DATA statement is a dummy.)

```
010 DATA 8, 11, 13, 17, 30, 33, 36, 1000
020 READ A
030 READ B
040 IF B = 1000 THEN 100
050 IF B>=A THEN 80
060 PRINT "NUMBERS OUT OF SEQUENCE"
070 GO TO 110
080 LET A = B
090 GO TO 30
100 PRINT "NUMBERS ARE IN SEQUENCE"
110 END
```

◆RUN

NUMBERS ARE IN SEQUENCE

If the numbers are out of sequence, such as in this next program, the program gives the output shown below.

```
010 DATA 8, 11, 13, 17, 4, 33, 36, 1000
020 READ A
030 READ B
040 IF B=1000 THEN 100
050 IF B>=A THEN 80
060 PRINT "NUMBERS OUT OF SEQUENCE"
070 GO TO 110
080 LET A = B
090 GO TO 30
100 PRINT "NUMBERS ARE IN SEQUENCE"
110 END
```

◆RUN

    NUMBERS OUT OF SEQUENCE

Note that the OUT OF SEQUENCE message is given even if only one number is out of sequence.

The next program tests sets of values A, B, and C to determine which of the trio is largest. (Assume each set is comprised of three *different* values.)

```
010 DATA 8, 7, 9, 5, 4, 3, 7, 19, 8, 1000, 0, 0
020 READ A,B,C
030 IF A = 1000 THEN 140
040 IF A>B THEN 100
050 IF B>C THEN 80
060 PRINT "C LARGEST"
070 GO TO 20
080 PRINT "B LARGEST"
090 GO TO 20
100 IF A>C THEN 120
110 GO TO 60
120 PRINT "A LARGEST"
130 GO TO 20
140 END

◆RUN


C LARGEST
A LARGEST
B LARGEST
```

The program gives three answers. It could give more if more than three sets of values were given.

EXERCISES

1. What does the IF statement do in a BASIC program?
2. What are the six relationships that one value may have with another in BASIC?
3. For what purpose is a dummy value used in a DATA statement?
4. How is a dummy value selected?
5. When a condition is tested with an IF statement, what does the program do if the condition is found to be "true"?
6. In Question 5, what does the program do if the condition is found to be "false"?
7. Study this IF statement:

   200 IF J > K THEN 350

   Where does the program go if J's value is 18 and K's value is 25?

8. Study this IF statement:

    350 IF M = Q GO TO 40

    Where does the program go if M's value is 83 and Q's value is 70?

9. What are the three forms that values used in an IF statement may take?

10. What two words may be used in place of THEN in an IF statement?

11. Write a program that reads a value found in the DATA statement. Call the value V. If V's value is greater than 5, have the program print "LARGE"; otherwise, have it print "SMALL". You may assume that the value in the DATA statement is not 5.

12. Write a program that determines which is greater:

    SIN (2.6) or COS (1.8).

    If the former is true, have the program print "LARGE"; otherwise, have it print "SMALL". You may assume that the two values are different.

13. Write a program that determines which value is largest: the sine of 2.6, the cosine of 1.7, or the natural logarithm of 8.3, and have it print the answer. You may assume that the three values are all different.

14. Write a program that finds which of four values read from the DATA statement is smallest. Have the program print that smallest value. The identity of the value does not need to be given. You may assume that the four values are all different.

15. Write the same program as in Question 14 except have the program tell which of the four values is smallest: first, second, third, or fourth.

LOOPS

A *loop* is a series of instructions in a program that are executed more than once. Typically, loop instructions are executed ten, twenty, thirty, or even more times. It's not unusual for loop instructions to be executed thousands of times.

You have already dealt with loops of a sort. Example:

```
010 DATA 8,9,7,6,5,1000
020 READ X
030 IF X=1000 THEN 60
040 PRINT X,X^2
050 GO TO 20
060 END

◆RUN
```

8	64
9	81
7	49
6	36
5	25

Several instructions are executed over and over until the dummy value (1000, in this example) is found. The loop then terminates.

Note the GO TO statement at line 050. A GO TO statement always causes an unconditional jump to the line number mentioned.   Here, GO TO 20 causes the program to jump to line 20 (020 is the same as 20 in BASIC).

Loops can be constructed in a number of ways.   One way is typified by the flowchart that follows.   (We haven't discussed flowcharts yet, but the ones in this chapter should be understandable without any formal training.)

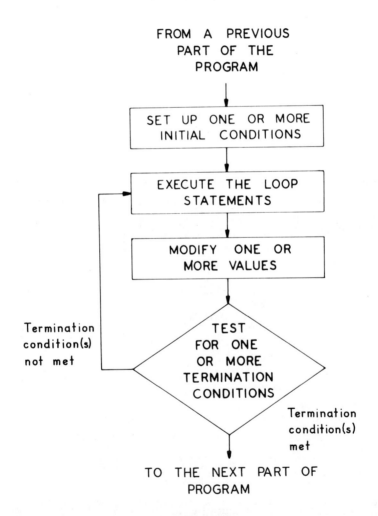

Figure 9-1

An example program that uses the flowchart is this:

```
010 LET C = 0
020 LET V = 1
030 PRINT V, V^2
040 LET V = V + .5
050 LET C = C + 1
060 IF V^2 > 75 THEN 80
070 GO TO 30
080 PRINT C
090 END
```

◆RUN

1	1
1.5	2.25
2	4
2.5	6.25
3	9
3.5	12.25
4	16
4.5	20.25
5	25
5.5	30.25
6	36
6.5	42.25
7	49
7.5	56.25
8	64
8.5	72.25
16	

The program sets initial conditions (LET C = 0 and LET V = 1). Then it executes the loop statement (PRINT V, V ↑ 2). Then, it modifies some values (LET V = V + .5 and LET C = C + 1), and finally checks whether a terminating condition has occurred. If the terminating condition has occurred, the program jumps to line 080; if not, the program returns to line 030, forming the loop. The terminating condition occurs when V^2 is greater than 75. (See line 060.) Just before the program terminates it prints the number of lines that were printed. C holds this information.

A user may rearrange some of the elements of the flowchart to suit himself or herself. For example, it may be desired to use the plan shown in the following flowchart.

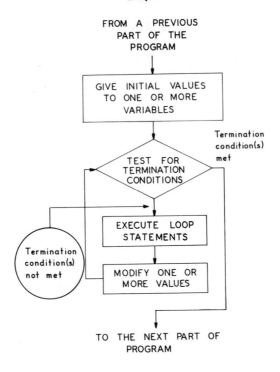

Figure 9-2

A program that agrees with the above flowchart is this:

```
010 LET X = 1.3
020 LET Y = 5.7
030 IF X + Y > 30 THEN 80
040 PRINT SIN(X), COS(Y), X,Y
050 LET X = X + .8
060 LET Y = Y + 1.01
070 GO TO 30
080 END
```

◆RUN

.9635582	.8347128	1.3	5.7
.8632094	.910289	2.1	6.71
.2392494	.1335812	2.9	7.72
-.5298361	-.7681958	3.7	8.73
-.9775301	-.9507276	4.5	9.74
-.8322675	-.2431135	5.3	10.75
-.1821627	.6921225	6.1	11.76
.5784396	.9793391	6.9	12.77
.9881682	.3496215	7.7	13.78
.7984873	-.6074392	8.5	14.79
.1244548	-.9957676	9.3	15.8
-.6250703	-.4517803	10.1	16.81
-.9954362	.5151992	10.9	17.82

Special cases of the general flowcharts given above arise when counters are established to count the number of times that a loop is to be executed. This next flowchart applies:

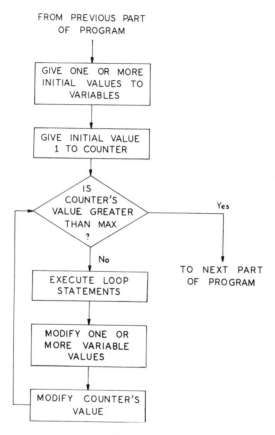

Figure 9-3

A program that agrees with the flowchart is shown below and on the following page.

```
010 LET A = 2.6
020 LET B = 9.7
030 LET C = 1
040 IF C > 6 THEN 100
050 PRINT A, LOG(A), B, LOG(B)
060 LET A = A + .3
070 LET B = B + .45
080 LET C = C + 1
090 GO TO 40
100 END
```

◆RUN

2.6	.9555114	9.7	2.272126
2.9	1.064711	10.15	2.317474
3.2	1.163151	10.6	2.360854
3.5	1.252763	11.05	2.40243
3.8	1.335001	11.5	2.442347
4.1	1.410987	11.95	2.480731

In this program, the name of the counter is C. When C's value exceeds 6, the program will stop. Six lines will be printed.

There are many more ways that a loop can be arranged. The user should be careful to plan a loop so that the statements in it are executed exactly the required number of times. (It is easy to make the kind of error that will cause the loop to be executed one more time than required or one less time.)

This next program gives a sum of all the integer numbers from 1 through 99.

```
010 LET S = 0
020 LET N = 1
030 IF N> 99 THEN 70
040 LET S = S + N
050 LET N = N + 1
060 GO TO 30
070 PRINT S
080 END
```

◆RUN

                    4950

The next program sums all the even integer numbers from 2 through 100.

```
010 LET S = 0
020 LET C = 2
030 IF C > 100 THEN 70
040 LET S = S + C
050 LET C = C + 2
060 GO TO 30
070 PRINT S
080 END
```

◆RUN

                    2550

This next program computes the approximate area under the sine curve from X = .5 to X = 2.5. To accomplish the task, the area is sliced into 100 vertical strips and the approximate area of each strip is computed. The areas of all 100 strips are summed.

```
010 LET T = 0
020 LET R = 2.5 - .5
030 LET W = R/100
040 LET M = W/2
050 LET X = .5 + M
060 LET C = 1
070 IF C > 100 THEN 130
080 LET A = W * SIN(X)
090 LET T = T + A
100 LET C = C + 1
110 LET X = X + W
120 GO TO 70
130 PRINT T
140 END

*RUN

    1.678754
```

The width of each vertical strip is W. The height of each strip is given by SIN(X). The height of each strip is measured at its midpoint. (See line numbers 040 and 050 where M represents half of a width and X represents the value at which point a height is computed.)

This area is not precisely accurate because a *rectangular* area is being measured but one side of each strip is not straight but curved. A better approximation of the area can be obtained by doubling the number of strips. Example:

```
010 LET T = 0
020 LET R = 2.5 - .5
030 LET W = R/200
040 LET M = W/2
050 LET X = .5 + M
060 LET C = 1
070 IF C > 200 THEN 130
080 LET A = W * SIN(X)
090 LET T = T + A
100 LET C = C + 1
110 LET X = X + W
120 GO TO 70
130 PRINT T
140 END

*RUN

    1.678733
```

and by redoubling:

```
010 LET T = 0
020 LET R = 2.5 - .5
030 LET W = R/400
040 LET M = W/2
050 LET X = .5 + M
060 LET C = 1
070 IF C > 400 THEN 130
080 LET A = W * SIN(X)
090 LET T = T + A
100 LET C = C + 1
110 LET X = X + W
120 GO TO 70
130 PRINT T
140 END
```

```
◆RUN
```

```
1.678727
```

Eventually, no great improvement in the result can be obtained by continuing to double the number of strips.

EXERCISES

1. Define the term *loop*.
2. Explain why the GO TO statement in BASIC is useful in setting up loops.
3. What BASIC command can be used to give initial conditions where a loop is being coded?
4. What BASIC command can be used to test for the termination condition(s) in a loop?
5. What is meant by the term *terminating condition(s)?*
6. What does a counter do where loops are being created and used?
7. Study this program:

```
10 READ V
20 PRINT V, V ↑ 2
30 GO TO 10
40 DATA 8,5,9,2
50 END
```

How many print lines will this program give besides the END OF DATA message?

8. Study this next program:

```
10 LET C = 1
20 LET V = 5
30 PRINT V, V ↑ 2
40 LET C = C + 1
50 LET V = V + 5
60 GO TO 30
70 END
```

What is the problem with the loop? How can the problem be solved?

9. Write a BASIC program that causes your name to be printed eight times.

10. Study this next program:

```
10 LET V = 5
20 IF V ↑ 2 > 230 THEN 60
30 PRINT V, V ↑ 2
40 LET V = V + 5
50 GO TO 20
60 END
```

How many print lines will this program give?

11. Write a program that computes and prints all the natural logarithms of V where V varies from 20.6 through 21.8 in steps of .2. Have the program also print V's value along with each logarithm.

12. Write a program that computes $1 + 2 + 3 + \cdots + 20$, that is, the sum of the integers from 1 through 20.

AUTOMATIC LOOPS

The FOR and NEXT statements can be used to simplify the formation of loops. Example:

```
010 FOR I = 1 TO 5
020 PRINT "TOM BROWN"
030 NEXT I
040 END

◆RUN

TOM BROWN
TOM BROWN
TOM BROWN
TOM BROWN
TOM BROWN
```

In this program, I is the name of a counter. It has been set to vary from 1 through 5 in steps of 1. The program prints TOM BROWN five times. Observe the placement of NEXT I. The loop consists of the three statements that begin with FOR I and end with NEXT I.

The next program prints the value of the counter as the loop is executed five times.

```
010 FOR I = 1 TO 5
020 PRINT I
030 NEXT I
040 END

◆RUN

            1
            2
            3
            4
            5
```

The following program gives a sum of the integer numbers from 1 through 5. Observe that S is initialized at zero. The value 1 is added to S, then 2, then 3, etc. When the program completes the loop, it prints the value of S. The sum of $1 + 2 + 3 + 4 + 5$ is 15.

```
010 LET S = 0
020 FOR I = 1 TO 5
030 LET S = S + I
040 NEXT I
050 PRINT S
060 END

◆RUN

            15
```

A simple change in the program at line 020 causes the summation of the integer numbers from 1 through 1000:

```
010 LET S = 0
020 FOR I = 1 TO 1000
030 LET S = S + I
040 NEXT I
050 PRINT S
060 END

◆RUN

            500500
```

Another change causes the values to be summed in steps of two. That is, the values summed are 1, 3, 5, 7, etc. The last value added to S is 999. The counter never exceeds the maximum value

shown in the FOR statement. In this example, the maximum value
is 1000.

```
010 LET S = 0
020 FOR I = 1 TO 1000 STEP 2
030 LET S = S + I
040 NEXT I
050 PRINT S
060 END

◆RUN

      250000
```

If we want a sum of the integer numbers from 2 through 1000
in steps of two, line 020 is changed as shown below. The last value
added to S is 1000.

```
010 LET S = 0
020 FOR I = 2 TO 1000 STEP 2
030 LET S = S + I
040 NEXT I
050 PRINT S
060 END

◆RUN

      250500
```

The step size can be any desired value. In the next example,
it is 7. When the program completes the loop, the program prints
the value of S and also the value of I. The value of I that is printed
tells what was the last value of I that was actually used inside the
loop.

```
010 LET S = 0
020 FOR I = 2 TO 1000 STEP 7
030 LET S = S + I
040 NEXT I
050 PRINT S
055 PRINT I
060 END

◆RUN

      71357
      996
```

This program computes the sum $2 + 9 + 16 + 23 + \ldots + 996$. That sum is 71357.

The beginning value of a counter may be negative. In the next program, I varies from -342 to 1000 in steps of 23. The last value added to S is 992.

```
010 LET S = 0
020 FOR I=-342 TO 1000 STEP 23
030 LET S = S + I
040 NEXT I
050 PRINT S
055 PRINT I
060 END

◆RUN

        19175
         992
```

The next example shows that values in a FOR statement need not always be integers (whole numbers). Here, the values added to S are -34.7, -34.6, -34.5, etc. Note that the step size, also, is not an integer. It is .1. The last value added to S is 43.8.

```
010 LET S = 0
020 FOR I=-34.7 TO 43.8 STEP .1
030 LET S = S + I
040 NEXT I
050 PRINT S
055 PRINT I
060 END

◆RUN

        3576.26
        43.79994
```

Because of a slight inaccuracy in the way that a computer stores .1 internally, the results shown above are slightly inaccurate. The two numbers should actually be 3576.3 and 43.8.

The next program reads ten values from the DATA statement and sums them. The name of each value read is X. Observe that this time the name of the counter is J. Any BASIC name can be assigned as the name of a counter.

```
010 DATA 3,8,5,2,3,7,6,5,1,9
020 LET S = 0
030 FOR J = 1 TO 10
040 READ X
050 LET S = S + X
060 NEXT J
070 PRINT S
080 END
```

◆RUN

                    49

A simple change to line 070 causes the average of the values,
as well as the sum, to be printed.

```
010 DATA 3,8,5,2,3,7,6,5,1,9
020 LET S = 0
030 FOR J = 1 TO 10
040 READ X
050 LET S = S + X
060 NEXT J
070 PRINT S,S/10
080 END
```

◆RUN

                    49   4.9

The sum of the values, S, and S divided by 10 is printed.
    The next program reads values from the DATA statement
until the dummy value 1000 is encountered. The loop, which has
been set up to execute a maximum of 100 times, is terminated
early. Observe that J counts the values that are added to S.

```
010 DATA 3,8,5,2,3,7,1000
020 LET S = 0
030 FOR J = 1 TO 100
040 READ X
050 IF X = 1000 THEN 80
060 LET S = S + X
070 NEXT J
080 PRINT S,S/(J-1)
090 END
```

◆RUN

                28   4.666667

The reason 1 is subtracted from J at line 080 is because J's value is too large by one unit when the program jumps to line 080. The count includes the read-in value of 1000, which was not actually added to S. The program prints the sum of the six values that were found ahead of 1000 (28) and divides 28 by 6, giving the average 4.666667.

The FOR statement has this form:

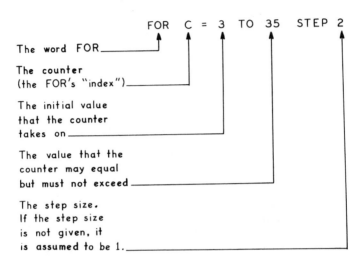

Here are some ways that FOR may be written:

```
FOR P = 10 TO 75
FOR Q = 30 TO 80 STEP 2
FOR R = -8 TO 700 STEP 9
FOR S = 80 TO -4 STEP -3   (Note the negative step size)
FOR T = -7.6 TO 8.4 STEP .3
FOR U = A TO B STEP C
FOR V = N TO W * R STEP (H + V)/F
```

A loop always extends from the FOR statement through the NEXT statement, like this:

```
100  FOR K = 1 TO 300
          .
          .
          .
          .
350  NEXT K
```

A program may leave a loop if necessary, like this:

```
300  FOR P = 1 TO 500
       .
       .
       .

500  IF W – T = 0 THEN 800
       .
       .
       .

600  NEXT P
       .
       .
       .

800  LET M = 3
       .
       .
       .
```

The important value remembered by the program after the exit from the loop is the value of the FOR's index. For example, if P's value is 86 when W – T = 0, the value 86 will be available to the program with the name P when the jump is made to line 800. Having left a loop, a program may return to the loop to complete it, if desired. To complete a loop, a jump must be made to the loop's NEXT statement. If a jump is made to the program's FOR statement, the loop begins again from the very beginning.

EXERCISES

1. What do statements that begin with the words FOR and NEXT accomplish in a BASIC program?

2. Study this FOR statement:

   ```
   FOR K = 1 TO 35
   ```

   What does K do?

3. What is the exact NEXT statement that you would give to match the FOR statement in Question 2.

4. How many statements may you place between the FOR statement in Question 2 and the NEXT statement in Question 3?

5. Study this statement:

    20 FOR I = 2 TO 1000 STEP 7

What is meant by the STEP 7 part of the statement?

6. Study the FOR statement in Question 5. How many different values will I take on that are actually used in the program?

7. Study this statement:

    20 FOR I = -342 TO 1000 STEP 23

What is the last value that I takes on that will actually be used in the program?

8. Is it possible for a step size in a program to be a fractional value such as .1? Are negative step sizes permitted? May step sizes be expressions such as (H + V) / F?

9. When a program exits from the range of a FOR/NEXT loop what important value is remembered by the program?

10. To what part of a FOR/NEXT loop must a program return if a loop is to be completed after an exit from the loop?

11. Study this program:

```
10 FOR K = 1 TO 50 STEP 3
20 PRINT "HELLO"
30 NEXT K
40 END
```

How many times will the computer system print HELLO?

12. Study this program:

```
10 DATA 6,8,9,2,14,7
20 READ X
30 IF X ↑ 2 > 80 THEN 50
40 GO TO 20
50 PRINT X
60 GO TO 20
70 END
```

How many print lines will the program give other than the END OF DATA message?

13. Write a program that computes the natural logarithm of V where V varies from 20.6 through 21.8 in steps of .2. Give V's value with each logarithm. Use a FOR/NEXT loop.

14. Write a program that computes the approximate area under the sine curve from X = .5 to X = 2.5. Use a FOR/NEXT loop.

11

ARRAYS AND SUBSCRIPTS

In this chapter, we introduce arrays and subscripts. An array is a group of related data values. For example, an array might consist of the final grades of 20 students in a math class. BASIC can work with arrays. As an example, the final grades mentioned above might be summed, or the highest grade might be found and printed. In order to work with an array, space must first be created for it; then values should be placed in the space.

The DIM statement is used to create space for arrays. Suppose, for example, we need five memory cells all named A (A_1, A_2, A_3, A_4, A_5). The DIM statement is used this way:

DIM A(5)

Five memory cells have been reserved. The memory cells look like this:

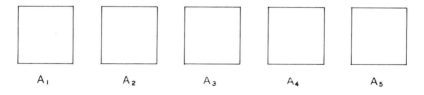

A_1 A_2 A_3 A_4 A_5

In BASIC, the word DIM is short for *dimension*. The dimension of A is 5. That is, the size of the array A is 5 memory cells.

Numbers can be loaded into an array with the use of the LET statement:

```
10 LET A(1) = 9
20 LET A(2) = 8
30 LET A(3) = 7
40 LET A(4) = 6
50 LET A(5) = 4
```

Array A now looks like this:

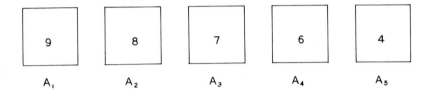

In each statement, the name of the array is given (A) and its location (1, 2, 3, etc.). The numbers inside the parentheses are called subscripts. A subscript indicates *which* cell of an array is being referenced.

Assignment statements may be all right to use when arrays are small, but when they are large—having 100, 1000, or more locations—data should be obtained from the DATA statement. Like this:

```
010 DIM A(5)
020 DATA 9,8,7,6,4
030 FOR J = 1 TO 5
040 READ A(J)
050 NEXT J
060 FOR K = 1 TO 5
070 PRINT A(K)
080 NEXT K
090 END

◆RUN

        9
        8
        7
        6
        4
```

The FOR and NEXT statements establish a loop that contains a READ statement. In the example, the subscript applying to A is

J. J cycles from 1 through 5. You can see that a subscript may be a name as well as an actual number. The loop executes five times, and the five values read from the DATA statement are stored in the array A like this:

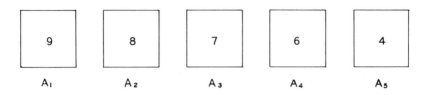

A_1 $\quad\quad\quad$ A_2 $\quad\quad\quad$ A_3 $\quad\quad\quad$ A_4 $\quad\quad\quad$ A_5

It's the same as if the program had included these READ statements:

```
READ A(1)
READ A(2)
READ A(3)
READ A(4)
READ A(5)
```

instead of the first FOR/NEXT loop.

The example program prints out the entire contents of array A. Observe that a subscript applying to an array does not always have to be the same name. The name J was used as the subscript name to read the array. The name K was used as the subscript name to print the array. Either name could have been used for either purpose.

The next example shows that a semicolon placed at the end of the PRINT statement causes all values to be printed on a line as space allows—additional lines might be needed for longer print-outs). Example:

```
010 DIM A(5)
020 DATA 9,8,7,6,4
030 FOR J = 1 TO 5
040 READ A(J)
050 NEXT J
060 FOR K = 1 TO 5
070 PRINT A(K);
080 NEXT K
090 END

◆RUN

     9    8    7    6    4
```

A comma can be placed at the end of a PRINT statement too. If used, a comma causes only five numbers to be printed per line.

The next program copies array A into array B. Note the key statement at line 070.

    70 LET B(K) = A(K)

The value of A_1 is assigned to B_1; the value of A_2 is assigned to B_2; etc. The values in the A array do not change. The program prints the entire contents of the A and B arrays.

```
010 DIM A(5),B(5)
020 DATA 9,8,7,6,4
030 FOR J = 1 TO 5
040 READ A(J)
050 NEXT J
060 FOR K = 1 TO 5
070 LET B(K) = A(K)
080 NEXT K
090 FOR K = 1 TO 5
100 PRINT A(K);B(K)
110 NEXT K
120 END

◆RUN

        9       9
        8       8
        7       7
        6       6
        4       4
```

The next program copies the A array into the B array in backwards order. The key statement is located at line 70.

    70 LET B(K) = A (6 - K)

K varies from 1 through 5. When K's value is 1, (6 - k)'s value is 5; when K's value is 2, (6 - K)'s value is 4; etc. It's the same as if the program had included these statements:

    LET B(1) = A(5)
    LET B(2) = A(4)
    LET B(3) = A(3)
    LET B(4) = A(2)
    LET B(5) = A(1)

instead of the second FOR/NEXT loop.

```
010 DIM A(5),B(5)
020 DATA 9,8,7,6,4
030 FOR J = 1 TO 5
040 READ A(J)
050 NEXT J
060 FOR K=1 TO 5
070 LET B(K)=A(6-K)
080 NEXT K
090 FOR K=1 TO 5
100 PRINT A(K);B(K)
110 NEXT K
120 END
```

◆RUN

```
9       4
8       6
7       7
6       8
4       9
```

The program shows that a subscript can be computed. See line 070.

We haven't said anything yet about when you would want to use an array. We'll discuss that question in depth in the next chapter. For now, let's examine a problem being solved two ways—first, without the use of an array and second, with the use of an array.

Let's assume we need to find the largest number in the DATA statement given in the next program.

```
010 DATA 3,5,6,4,2,8,7,4,6,1,1000
020 READ X
030 READ Y
040 IF Y=1000 THEN 90
050 IF Y>X THEN 70
060 GO TO 30
070 LET X=Y
080 GO TO 30
090 PRINT X
100 END
```

◆RUN

X holds the largest number. As the program runs, any value read that is larger than the *current* value of X is placed in X. The number 1000 at the end of the DATA values is a dummy. Its only function is to signal the end of the DATA.

If we assume that it is known that there are ten values in the DATA statement, the program to find the largest value could be written this way:

```
010 DATA 3,5,6,4,2,8,7,4,6,1
020 DIM A(10)
030 FOR N=1 TO 10
040 READ A(N)
050 NEXT N
060 LET B=A(1)
070 FOR J=2 TO 10
080 IF A(J)>B THEN 100
090 GO TO 110
100 LET B=A(J)
110 NEXT J
120 PRINT B
130 END

◆RUN

                    8
```

First, 10 values are read into the A array, then the value at A_1 is assigned to B. Next, the program examines all the remaining values of array A to find any that might be larger than B. When a value in the array is found to contain a value larger than the current value assigned to B, the program replaces B with that value. At the end of the program, the value of B is printed. This is the largest value.

If it had not been shown how many values there were in the DATA statement, a dummy could have been used to signal the end of the DATA values. Note this next example:

```
010 DATA 3,5,6,4,2,8,7,4,6,1,1000
020 DIM A(100)
030 FOR N = 1 TO 100
040 READ X
050 IF X = 1000 THEN 80
060 LET A(N) = X
070 NEXT N
080 LET B = A(1)
090 FOR J = 2 TO N-1
100 IF A(J) > B THEN 120
110 GO TO 130
```

```
120 LET B = A(J)
130 NEXT J
140 PRINT B
150 END

◆RUN

             8
```

Observe that the array defined in the DIM statement is now much larger and that the loop beginning at line 30 is set for more cycles. This program can handle a maximum of 99 values read from the DATA statement. The dummy value is the 100th, but that value is, of course, not used. Also observe that the FOR statement has been changed so that J varies from 2 through N-1, not 2 through 10 as before. N-1 holds a count of the numbers that were read from the DATA statement. The dummy value, 1000, *is* included in the count representing N. Reducing N by 1 means that the dummy value will be ignored in the search for the largest value.

The next program finds the largest value in the A array and also finds its position (location) within the array. The name L holds that position.

```
010 DATA 3,5,6,4,2,8,7,4,6,1
020 DIM A(10)
030 FOR N = 1 TO 10
040 READ A(N)
050 NEXT N
060 LET B=A(1)
065 LET L=1
070 FOR J=2 TO 10
080 IF A(J)>B THEN 100
090 GO TO 110
100 LET B=A(J)
105 LET L=J
110 NEXT J
120 PRINT B;L
130 END

◆RUN

       8     6
```

The largest value is 8, and its position in the A array is 6. Line 65 is necessary in this program because the largest value in the array might be the first one. At line 070, only the second through the tenth values of the array are examined because the first value has already been assigned to B.

The next program prints the values in the A array in decreasing sequence. To do this, the program finds the largest value, prints it, and then finds the next largest value and prints it, etc. Whenever a large value has been found and printed, it is changed to -5000 so that it will not appear as a largest value again. Note the key statement at line 121:

        121 LET A(L) = -5000

The name L holds the position (location) in the A array of the largest value found. That position number is used as a subscript for the A array. The largest value found is changed to a very small value.

```
010 DATA 3,5,6,4,2,8,7,4,6,1
020 DIM A(10)
030 FOR N = 1 TO 10
040 READ A(N)
050 NEXT N
055 FOR K=1 TO 10
060 LET B=A(1)
065 LET L=1
070 FOR J=2 TO 10
080 IF A(J)>B THEN 100
090 GO TO 110
100 LET B=A(J)
105 LET L=J
110 NEXT J
120 PRINT B;L
121 LET A(L)=-5000
125 NEXT K
130 END

◆RUN

    8        6
    7        7
    6        3
    6        9
    5        2
    4        4
    4        8
    3        1
    2        5
    1       10
```

The numbers in the lefthand column are the sorted values in decreasing sequence; the numbers in the righthand column are their original positions in the A array.

The next program does not immediately print the largest values as they are found. Instead, the program stores them in the X array, then prints all of the X array at one time.

```
010 DATA 3,5,6,4,2,8,7,4,6,1
020 DIM A(10),X(10)
030 FOR N = 1 TO 10
040 READ A(N)
050 NEXT N
055 FOR K=1 TO 10
060 LET B=A(1)
065 LET L=1
070 FOR J=2 TO 10
080 IF A(J)>B THEN 100
090 GO TO 110
100 LET B=A(J)
105 LET L=J
110 NEXT J
120 LET X(K)=B
121 LET A(L)=-5000
125 NEXT K
130 FOR W = 1 TO 10
140 PRINT X(W);
150 NEXT W
160 END

◆RUN

    8    7    6    6    5    4    4    3    2    1
```

A few changes to the program cause it to sort the values in increasing rather than decreasing sequence. Observe the changes to lines 080 and 121:

```
010 DATA 3,5,6,4,2,8,7,4,6,1
020 DIM A(10),X(10)
030 FOR N = 1 TO 10
040 READ A(N)
050 NEXT N
055 FOR K=1 TO 10
060 LET B=A(1)
065 LET L=1
070 FOR J=2 TO 10
080 IF A(J)<B THEN 100
090 GO TO 110
100 LET B=A(J)
105 LET L=J
110 NEXT J
120 LET X(K)=B
121 LET A(L)=5000
125 NEXT K
130 FOR W=1 TO 10
140 PRINT X(W);
150 NEXT W
160 END

◆RUN

    1    2    3    4    4    5    6    6    7    8
```

EXERCISES

1. What does the DIM statement accomplish in a BASIC program?
2. Define the term *subscript*.
3. Give the BASIC statement that assigns the value 21.8 to the seventh location of the array named W.
4. Why should a FOR/NEXT loop be used to assign values to a large array?
5. What are the three forms that subscripts may take?
6. What does a dummy value located at the end of a DATA statement accomplish?
7. Study this program segment:

```
10 DIM   X(200)
20 FOR   L = 1 TO 200
30 LET   X(L) = -1
40 NEXT L
     .
     .
     .
```

   What has the program stored in all 200 locations of the array X?
8. Study this program segment:

```
10 DIM Y(200)
20 FOR K = 1 TO 200
30 LET Y(K) = K
40 NEXT K
     .
     .
     .
```

   What has the program stored in the 200 locations of the array Y?
9. Study the program segment on the next page.

```
10 DATA 8,7,4,9,2,4
20 DIM A(6), B(6)
30 FOR K = 1 TO 6
40 READ A(K)
50 LET B(K) = A(K)
60 NEXT K
    .
    .
    .
```

What is in the A and B arrays at this time?

10. Study this program segment:

```
10 DATA 5,4,9,8,6
20 DIM    F(5)
30 READ F(1)
40 READ F(2)
50 READ F(3)
60 READ F(4)
70 READ F(5)
    .
    .
    .
```

Rewrite the program segment so that it accomplishes the same objective but uses FOR/NEXT statements and a READ statement rather than the five READs shown above.

11. Write a program that puts a zero in every element of an X array having a dimension of 20. Have the program print the array.

12. Refer to Question 11. Have the program put the values 2, 4, 6, 8, . . . etc., in the array. Have the program print the array.

FLOWCHARTING

When problems are simple, the procedures for solving the problems are also simple, and programmers can probably hold entire procedures in their minds as they write the programs.

Suppose, for example, you want to write a program that gives the square root of all whole numbers from 1 through 10. The procedure, easily defined, is to use a FOR/NEXT loop where the counter in the loop also serves as the actual argument for the SQR function. The BASIC program is:

```
10 FOR K = 1 TO 10
20 PRINT SQR(K)
30 NEXT K
40 END
```

There is no difficulty in understanding the problem, understanding how it is to be solved, and understanding the program once it has been written. Not all problems are this simple.

Suppose it is necessary to obtain two numbers from the DATA statement (A and B); determine which is larger, the first or the second; and then print A – B if A is larger than B or print A + B if A is smaller than B. If A equals B, the program is to give an error message. This problem is more complex than the first but can still be solved without a great deal of difficulty, as shown on the next page.

```
010 DATA 8,4
020 READ A,B
030 IF A > B THEN 70
040 IF A = B THEN 90
050 PRINT A + B
060 GO TO 100
070 PRINT A - B
080 GO TO 100
090 PRINT "ERROR IN DATA"
100 END

◆RUN
```

4

With a little experience, even a beginner can devise a procedure for solving a simple problem, then sit at a terminal and enter the program.

But eventually, the programmer must work on a problem that is complex. For example, a programmer may need to enter twenty numbers into an array, then have the computer sort them and print them in increasing sequence. If the programmer tries to develop the procedure for solving the problem and retain it in the mind while entering the program, he or she may become confused. The person may give some of the steps in incorrect order or, worse, may leave out some necessary steps. A programmer should use a flowchart as a programming and debugging aid.

What is a flowchart? How does one learn to flowchart? A flowchart is a pictorial guide that a programmer uses when he or she plans the procedure for solving a problem. The guide gives the step-by-step procedure that the program must follow when obtaining the solution to the problem. Once developed and thoroughly checked, the flowchart provides an excellent guide for the programmer. The program almost writes itself. The programmer does not have to worry about giving the procedure in an incorrect sequence because the flowchart precisely defines the correct sequence. The person does not have to worry about leaving out a step because the flowchart gives *every* step.

Let's discuss flowcharting by starting out with some very simple problems. Suppose a programmer wishes to compute 35 X 834 and print the result. The flowchart for the program is this:

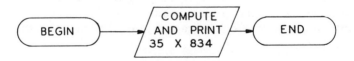

The BASIC program that conforms to this flowchart is:

```
10 PRINT 35 * 834
20 END
```

Examine the flowchart. It has three symbols:

The oval is used for only two purposes: to define the beginning point of a flowchart and to show the termination point of the flowchart. The only words you'll ever see in ovals are BEGIN and END (or other words that mean the same as BEGIN and END). Arrows in a flowchart define the *flow* of the solution procedure. They define the sequence of the instructions that are given. The BEGIN oval is usually located in the upper lefthand corner of the first sheet that contains the flowchart. The END oval could be located anywhere on any sheet of the flowchart. (Flowcharts can sometimes be given completely on a single sheet of paper; sometimes they extend over many sheets.)

The parallelogram ⟋▭⟋ in the flowchart is used for operations involving input and output operations. Therefore, one would expect the words READ and PRINT to be associated with the input/output (I/O) symbol.

Admittedly, the flowchart given above and its associated problem solution are extremely simple. But, we must learn to creep before we can run. Let's move a little faster. Study this flowchart:

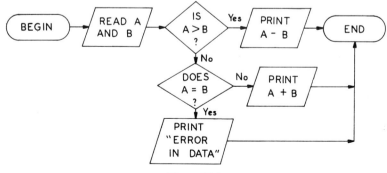

Figure 12-1

The program that conforms to this flowchart is:

```
010 DATA 8,4
020 READ A,B
030 IF A > B THEN 70
040 IF A = B THEN 90
050 PRINT A + B
060 GO TO 100
070 PRINT A - B
080 GO TO 100
090 PRINT "ERROR IN DATA"
100 END

◆RUN

4
```

This flowchart introduces the decision diamond. It is used where you want a program to decide between alternate courses of action. Observe that the first decision diamond

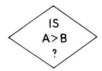

asks a question: Is A > B? If the answer is "yes," the YES arrow flowing out of the diamond tells what has to be done next; if the answer is "no," the NO arrow flowing out of the diamond tells what has to be done next. The YES and NO arrows may flow out of a diamond in any direction that the programmer selects. He or she usually chooses directions that keep lines short or that help make the flowchart attractive.

In a BASIC program the YES path is always the THEN path, and the NO path is always to the statement that immediately follows the IF. In this sequence:

```
30 IF A > B THEN 70

40 IF A = B THEN 90

50 PRINT A + B
```

the program checks A to determine whether it is greater than B. If the answer is "yes," the program jumps to line 70, if the answer is "no," the program goes to the next statement (line 40). At line 40, the program gives another IF statement. If A equals B the program is to go to line 90 to give an error message; otherwise, it is to print A + B. Observe that, if A is not greater than B, *and* it is not equal to B, then it must be less than B. The value A + B is to be printed when A is less than B.

When writing a flowchart, one is not concerned with the BASIC program that is to be written from the flowchart. The primary concern is "Does the flowchart do what it is supposed to do?" If the answer is "yes," the flowchart is completed. If the answer is "no," the flowchart must be modified until it does accomplish its objective.

Considerable trial and error may be involved when a flowchart is being developed. Tentative approaches to the problem solution may be attempted and rejected. Even the correct approach, once discovered, may have to be changed as the flowchart is developed. You should not be alarmed if you find yourself spending a great deal of time on the development of a flowchart. This is perfectly normal. Most of the effort in the solution of a problem *should* be devoted to the flowchart. As we said, when the flowchart is correct, the final BASIC program almost writes itself.

A programmer should not worry about what he or she writes within the flowchart symbols. Ordinary English is used. For example, suppose the programmer wishes to interrogate A to see if it's greater than B. The programmer can give decision diamonds like these:

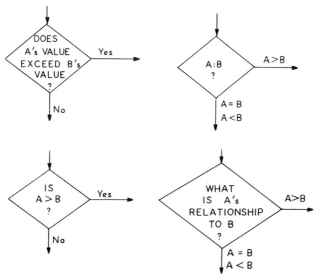

Figure 12-2

There is usually no right or wrong way to write a flowchart. If a flowchart guides the programmer toward the desired goal and is easily understood by others, then it can be said that the flowchart is correct. For guidance, you might want to pattern your flowcharts after the ones shown in this chapter.

Having developed a flowchart, convert it to a BASIC program by beginning at the point labeled BEGIN. Then follow the arrows and write BASIC statements that agree with the flowchart symbols. When a decision diamond is encountered, write the IF statement, then follow the NO path of the flowchart. When all NO paths in the main flow of the flowchart have been processed, select any YES path and follow that one, etc. Let's try an example:

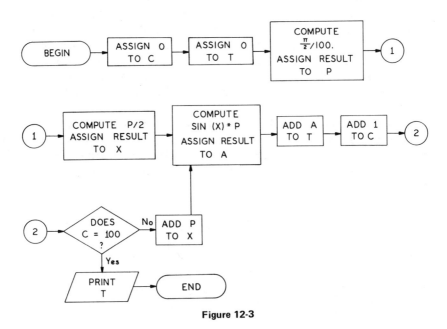

Figure 12-3

This flowchart introduces two more flowcharting symbols:

These are the assignment and connector symbols, respectively. The assignment symbol is used in connection with LET statements.

For example, "ASSIGN 0 TO X" would be expressed in BASIC as LET X = 0. Also, "COMPUTE $\frac{\pi}{2}$/100. ASSIGN RESULT TO P" would be expressed in BASIC as LET P = (3.1416/2)/100. The connector symbol is used to eliminate lines between one part of the flowchart and another. In the example, the connector symbol makes it possible to eliminate the line leading from ──▸① to ①──▸ and ──▸② to ②──▸ . Connector symbols may also be used to connect a flowchart from one page to another. For example, you might give this in a flowchart:

──▸⟨20⟩ To Page 5

and this:

From Page 3 ──▸⟨20⟩

In writing the BASIC program that conforms to the flowchart shown above, one begins at the symbol (BEGIN). There is no BASIC statement that corresponds to this symbol, so none is used. Following the arrow we come to

```
ASSIGN
0  TO  C
```

The symbol translates to:

    10 LET C = 0

Next, the symbol:

```
ASSIGN  0
  TO  T
```

converts to:

      20 LET T = 0

So it goes until our program looks like this:

      10 LET C = 0
      20 LET T = 0
      30 LET P = (3.1416/2)/100
      40 LET X = P/2
      50 LET A = SIN(X)*P
      60 LET T = T + A
      70 LET C = C + 1

We now have the symbol:

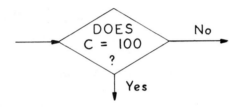

The IF statement is this:

      80 IF C = 100 THEN

We don't know what line number to use following THEN, so we
leave it out until we have taken care of the NO path out of the IF.
The flowchart shows the NO path leading to the symbol:

```
ADD   P
TO   X
```

Therefore, at line 90, we write

      90 LET X = X + P

An arrow leading from the symbol shown above to another symbol
indicates that a GO TO must be given in the program—to the point

where the value of A is computed. Therefore, at line 100, we give
this command:

100 GO TO 50

Line 110 is now available to us to use as the line number following
THEN in line 80. So we add 110 to the IF statement giving:

80 IF C = 100 THEN 110

Now we can complete the program by giving the PRINT statement
that has to appear at line 110, followed by the END statement.
Like this:

110 PRINT T

120 END

The complete program, along with the output from a run, looks
like this:

```
010 LET C = 0
020 LET T = 0
030 LET P = (3.1416/2)/100
040 LET X = P/2
050 LET A = SIN(X)*P
060 LET T = T + A
070 LET C = C + 1
080 IF C = 100 THEN 110
090 LET X = X + P
100 GO TO 50
110 PRINT T
120 END

*RUN

      1.000014
```

This program was written without our even having to understand what the program does. This is possible when a flowchart
has been written well. (The program computes the approximate
area under the sine curve from X = 0 TO X = $\frac{\pi}{2}$.)

Once a program has been debugged, an excellent documentation practice is to return to the flowchart and jot down, next to
the corresponding flowchart symbols, the line numbers of key por-
tions of the program, as shown on the next page.

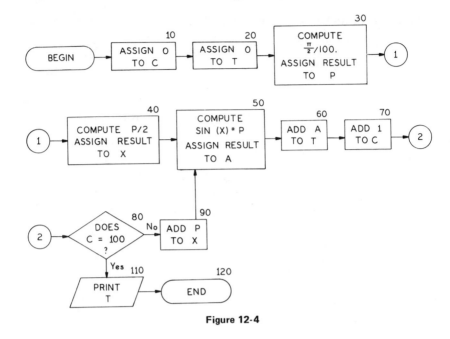

Figure 12-4

If a program uses a FOR/NEXT loop, one way to indicate a loop is this:

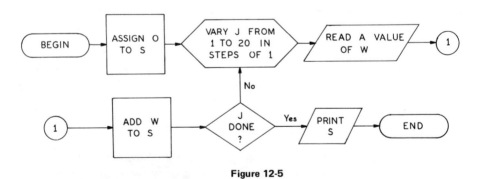

Figure 12-5

The following program sums 20 values read from a data statement:

```
010 LET S = 0
020 FOR J = 1 TO 20
030 READ W
040 LET S = S + W
050 NEXT J
060 PRINT S
070 DATA 7,4,9,8,4,3,6,1,8,3,4,6,9,1,4,6,7,4,9,6
080 END
```

◆RUN

109

Sometimes it is better to orient a flowchart vertically rather than horizontally. One reason that we might want to write the above flowchart vertically is so that the loop is recognizable more readily. Note:

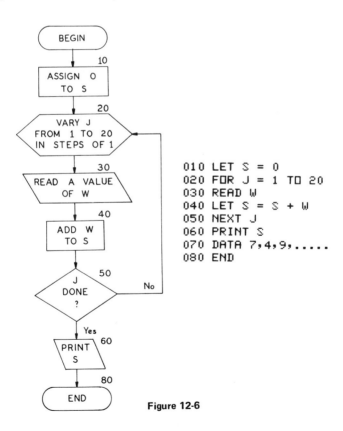

```
010 LET S = 0
020 FOR J = 1 TO 20
030 READ W
040 LET S = S + W
050 NEXT J
060 PRINT S
070 DATA 7,4,9,.....
080 END
```

Figure 12-6

A FOR/NEXT loop within another FOR/NEXT loop can be designated as shown below:

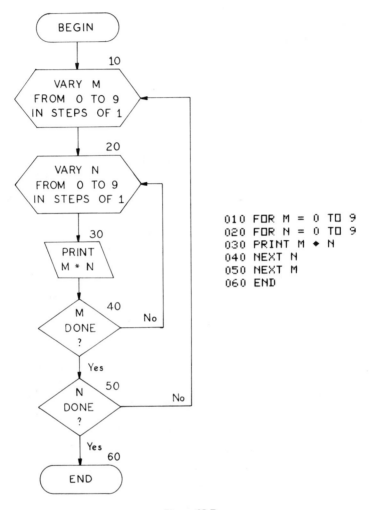

```
010 FOR M = 0 TO 9
020 FOR N = 0 TO 9
030 PRINT M * N
040 NEXT N
050 NEXT M
060 END
```

Figure 12-7

The program above prints all possible products using values of M and N varying M and N from 0 through 9 (100 products).

If variables require subscripts, the flowchart can show them in engineering or in BASIC notation. For example, a segment of a program that searches the H array for the largest value may be written in either of the two ways shown in Figure 12-8.

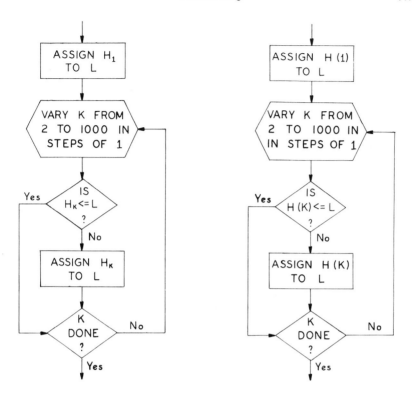

Figure 12-8

When the program leaves the FOR/NEXT loop, the variable L holds the largest value found in the 1000-element H array.

Mastering flowcharting is not something you will achieve in an hour or so of study. To become proficient, you must practice. From this point, when you plan the solution to a computer problem, make it a habit to flowchart first. You will be surprised at how readily you master the technique and begin to use it effectively in your work.

EXERCISES

1. What is a flowchart?
2. When should a flowchart be used?

3. Why is it true that, when a flowchart has been completely defined, the BASIC program almost writes itself?

4. In a flowchart, what does the oval represent?

5. In a flowchart, what does a parallelogram represent?

6. What are the only two words (or equivalent) that you might ever see in a flowchart parallelogram?

7. What are the only two words (or equivalent) that you might ever see in a flowchart oval?

8. In a flowchart, what does the diamond represent?

9. How are the arrows flowing out of a decision diamond labelled?

10. What is the important consideration about what one writes in a flowchart symbol?

11. In a flowchart, what does the rectangle represent?

12. In a flowchart, what does the small circle represent?

13. May flowcharts be oriented vertically as well as horizontally?

14. How can you learn to flowchart effectively in the shortest possible time?

15. Give the flowchart for the program that follows:

```
10 LET R = 4.37
20 LET T = 9.47
30 LET A = R * T
40 PRINT A,T,R
50 END
```

16. Give the flowchart for the program that follows:

```
10 DATA 7,9,4,8
20 READ F
30 PRINT F, F ↑ 2
40 GO TO 20
50 END
```

17. Give the flowchart for the program that follows:

```
10 DATA 9,4,7,8,1000
20 READ H
30 IF H = 1000 THEN 60
40 PRINT H, H ↑ 2
50 GO TO 20
60 PRINT "END REPORT"
70 END
```

18. Give the flowchart for the program that follows:

```
10 FOR L = 1 TO 20
20 PRINT "ALL DONE"
30 NEXT L
40 END
```

19. Write a program that corresponds with this flowchart:

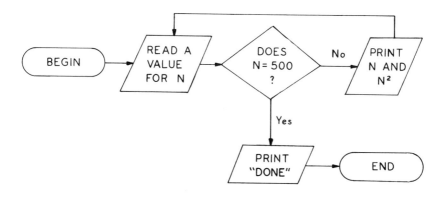

20. Write a program that corresponds with the flowchart on page 120. K represents employee number; H, hours worked; R, pay rate; P, gross pay.

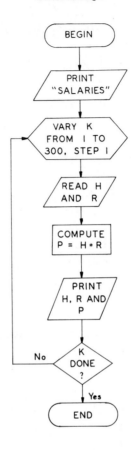

DEBUGGING

Programs don't always run correctly the first time they are tried. If a program doesn't work properly, it has to be debugged. That is, errors must be eliminated from the program. Let's observe how debugging can be done.

In this next program the programmer wants to compare A and B. If A's value is larger than B's value, the individual wants to assign 32.9 to C and print A, B, and C. If A's value is not greater than B's value, he or she wants to assign 45.6 to C and print A, B, and C. The programmer has not only written a poor program (the task is not really suited for computer solution), but he or she has also made many errors. The printout is shown below and on the next page.

```
010 LET A=3.4.6
020 LEX B=94.6
030 IF A>B THEN GO TO 500
040 LET CX=45.6
050 GO TO 600
500 LET C=32.9-
510 PRINT A;B;C
520 END


◆RUN
010 LET A=3.4.6
              ^
STATEMENT ERROR
020 LEX B=94.6
        ^
```

```
STATEMENT ERROR
030 IF A>B THEN GO TO 500
                   ^

STATEMENT ERROR
040 LET CX=45.6
        ^

STATEMENT ERROR
500 LET C=32.9-
              ^

STATEMENT ERROR
NO LINE NUMBER   600
```

The computer system has identified several errors and notified the user. The error messages are given after the user types RUN.

The programmer corrects the statements at lines 010, 020, and 030, then requests a list and a run again.

```
010 LET A=34.6
020 LET B=94.6
030 IF A>B THEN 500
LIST


010 LET A=34.6
020 LET B=94.6
030 IF A>B THEN 500
040 LET CX=45.6
050 GO TO 600
500 LET C=32.9-
510 PRINT A;B;C
520 END


*RUN
040 LET CX=45.6
        ^

STATEMENT ERROR
500 LET C=32.9-
              ^

STATEMENT ERROR
NO LINE NUMBER   600
```

There are still some errors. The individual corrects the statements at lines 040 and 050, then tries again:

```
040 LET C=45.6
050 GO TO 500
LIST


010 LET A=34.6
020 LET B=94.6
030 IF A>B THEN 500
040 LET C=45.6
050 GO TO 510
500 LET C=32.9-
510 PRINT A;B;C
520 END


◆RUN
500 LET C=32.9-
                  ^
STATEMENT ERROR
```

There is still an error. The user corrects the error, then tries once more. Correct answers are given this time.

```
500 LET C=-32.9
LIST

010 LET A=34.6
020 LET B=94.6
030 IF A>B THEN 500
040 LET C=45.6
050 GO TO 510
500 LET C=-32.9
510 PRINT A;B;C
520 END

◆RUN

34.6   94.6   45.6
```

This programmer would now like to sum all the even integers from 2 through 100. He or she writes the next program and gets the answer 198.

```
010 LET S=0
020 FOR J=2 TO 100
030 LET S=S+2
040 NEXT J
050 PRINT S
060 END

◆RUN

            198
```

Realizing that the answer is wrong (it has to be much larger), the individual changes the program at line 020 and tries again. This time the result is worse:

```
010 LET S=0
020 FOR J=2 TO 100 STEP 2
030 LET S=S+2
040 NEXT J
050 PRINT S
060 END

◆RUN

            100
```

The programmer now inserts a PRINT statement at line 035 so that he or she can see what's happening to S as the program executes. This is the printout:

```
010 LET S=0
020 FOR J=2 TO 100 STEP 2
030 LET S=S+2
035 PRINT S;
040 NEXT J
050 PRINT S
060 END

◆RUN
```

2	4	6	8	10	12	14	16	18	20	22	24
26	28	30	32	34	36	38	40	42	44	46	48
50	52	54	56	58	60	62	64	66	68	70	72
74	76	78	80	82	84	86	88	90	92	94	96
98	100	100									

The user observes that S is growing too slowly. It should be growing this way:

2, 6, 12, 20, etc.

Mistakenly, the individual changes line 030 from

    030 LET S = S + 2

to

    030 LET S = S + S

but the results are no better. (S's value is initially set to zero at line 020 and it never changes.) Here is the printout:

```
010 LET S=0
020 FOR J=2 TO 100 STEP 2
030 LET S=S+S
035 PRINT S;
040 NEXT J
050 PRINT S
060 END

◆RUN
```

```
    0      0      0      0      0      0      0      0      0      0      0      0
    0      0      0      0      0      0      0      0      0      0      0      0
    0      0      0      0      0      0      0      0      0      0      0      0
    0      0      0      0      0      0      0      0      0      0      0      0
    0      0      0
```

The programmer realizes that line 030 should read

    030 LET S = S + J

The program now appears to operate properly. Note the printout that follows:

```
010 LET S=0
020 FOR J=2 TO 100 STEP 2
030 LET S=S+J
035 PRINT S;
040 NEXT J
050 PRINT S
060 END

◆RUN
```

2	6	12	20	30	42	56	72	90	110	132	156
182	210	240	272	306	342	380	420	462	506	552	600
650	702	756	812	870	930	992	1056	1122	1190	1260	1332
1406	1482	1560	1640	1722	1806	1892	1980	2070	2162	2256	2352
2450	2550	2550									

J's initial value is 2. The FOR statement changes it to 4, then 6, then 8, etc. Every J value from 2 through 100 is added to 5 within the FOR/NEXT loop. After the loop has been completed, S contains the required answer.

The programmer's final action is to remove the PRINT statement at line 035 and rerun the program one final time:

```
010 LET S=0
020 FOR J=2 TO 100 STEP 2
030 LET S=S+J
040 NEXT J
050 PRINT S
060 END

◆RUN

      2550
```

Inserting extra PRINT statements in a program can help you find out why a program isn't operating correctly. The PRINT statements can be removed after the program has been debugged.

There are so many kinds of errors that programmers might make that categorizing them is difficult. Some types are these:

1. The programmer spells a key word incorrectly. For example, PRINT might be spelled PIRNT.
2. A key word is omitted. The command FOR J = 2 TO 100 step 2 might be mistakenly given as FOR J = 2, 100, step 2.
3. A FOR might be given without a matching NEXT, or vice versa.
4. A statement type might be confused with another. For example, LET J = 2 TO 100 step 2 is incorrect because the word LET has been confused with FOR.

The student should realize that errors are easy to make. He or she should not become discouraged. We all learn from our mistakes.

EXERCISES

1. What is meant by the term *debugging?*
2. When does the timesharing system tell you that you have made one or more clerical mistakes in writing BASIC statements?

3. How does one correct errors in BASIC statements?

4. How can extra PRINT statements in a program help debug the program? What should happen to these PRINT statements after the program is operating properly?

5. Study this program and tell what's wrong with it.

```
10 LEM B = 4
20 GET R = 1
30 PRINT B,R
40 END
```

6. Study this program and tell what's wrong with it.

```
10 FOR L = -1 TO 50 STEP -1
20 PRINT "TEST"
30 NEXT L
40 END
```

7. Study this program and tell what's wrong with it.

```
10 READ E
20 PRINT E, E ↑ 2
30 GO TO 10
40 END
50 DATA 9,7,4,8
```

8. Study this program and tell what's wrong with it.

```
10 FOR D = 1 TO 10
20 PRINT "TEST"
30 FOR E = 1 TO 5
40 PRINT "HELLO"
50 NEXT D
60 NEXT E
70 END
```

THE INPUT STATEMENT

The INPUT statement can be used in place of READ for a more interactive mode of operation between a user and the computer system. Interactive means that the user and the computer contact each other frequently during the solution of a problem. Consider this example:

```
010 INPUT X
020 PRINT X,X^2,X^3
030 GO TO 10
040 END

◆RUN

?4.5
            4.5            20.25            91.125
?-8
            -8             64               -512
?STOP
```

When the computer encounters the INPUT statement, it types a question mark. The user types one or more values and the program continues. In the example above, the computer requests a number (X), then prints the number, its square, and its cube. The system then asks for another number, and the procedure is repeated. The user stops the program by typing STOP.

The program can be designed to tell the user what he or she is expected to enter. Example:

```
005 PRINT "ENTER A NUMBER WHEN SYSTEM TYPES QUESTION MARK"
006 PRINT "PROGRAM STOPS WHEN YOU ENTER ZERO"
010 INPUT X
015 IF X=0 THEN 40
020 PRINT X,X^2,X^3
030 GO TO 10
040 END

◆RUN

ENTER A NUMBER WHEN SYSTEM TYPES QUESTION MARK
PROGRAM STOPS WHEN YOU ENTER ZERO
?5.6
        5.6             31.36          175.616
?-8
        -8              64             -512
?0
```

Observe that the program is self-terminating. In this example, when the user gives zero, the program jumps to the END statement. The next example shows that the computer system has certain built-in error checks that the user does not have to program. Note what happens when the user requests the square root of a negative number.

```
010 PRINT "THIS PROGRAM GIVES SQUARE ROOTS"
020 PRINT "ENTER '0' WHEN DONE"
030 PRINT "PLEASE ENTER A NUMBER"
040 INPUT X
050 IF X=0 THEN 80
060 PRINT X,SQR(X)
070 GO TO 30
080 END

◆RUN

THIS PROGRAM GIVES SQUARE ROOTS
ENTER '0' WHEN DONE
PLEASE ENTER A NUMBER
?6.7
        6.7         2.588436
PLEASE ENTER A NUMBER
?88.5
        88.5        9.407444
PLEASE ENTER A NUMBER
?123.456
        123.456         11.11108
PLEASE ENTER A NUMBER
?-45
        -45
IN 60   SQR(-N)ILLEGAL, EVAL FOR N
        6.708204
PLEASE ENTER A NUMBER
?0
```

The user can build in error checks, of course. In this next program, note the statements at lines 045 and 080.

```
010 PRINT "THIS PROGRAM GIVES SQUARE ROOTS"
020 PRINT "ENTER '0' WHEN DONE"
030 PRINT "PLEASE ENTER A NUMBER"
040 INPUT X
045 IF X<0 THEN 80
050 IF X=0 THEN 100
060 PRINT X,SQR(X)
070 GO TO 30
080 PRINT "CAN'T GIVE SQR OF NEG NUM."
090 GO TO 30
100 END

◆RUN

THIS PROGRAM GIVES SQUARE ROOTS
ENTER '0' WHEN DONE
PLEASE ENTER A NUMBER
?5.6
        5.6        2.366432
PLEASE ENTER A NUMBER
?-3
CAN'T GIVE SQR OF NEG NUM.
PLEASE ENTER A NUMBER
?0
```

Observe that the program tests the value entered to determine whether it can be used.

An INPUT statement can request more than one value:

```
010 INPUT X, Y, Z
020 PRINT X, Y, Z, X+Y+Z
030 GO TO 10
040 END

◆RUN


?3,6,9
        3           6           9
                                        18
?5,2,8
        5           2           8
                                        15
?STOP
```

The input statement has the form shown on the next page.

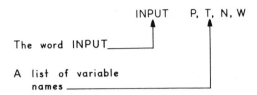

If a program requires more than one value, the user must type exactly the number of values requested. Typing fewer than the required numbers or more, will cause the computer system to report that an error has been made. The user can, of course, have the program print a message in advance telling what is expected.

Values can be read into arrays using INPUT. Example:

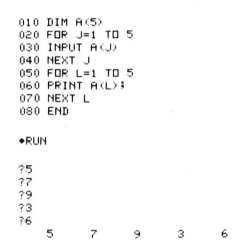

```
010 DIM A(5)
020 FOR J=1 TO 5
030 INPUT A(J)
040 NEXT J
050 FOR L=1 TO 5
060 PRINT A(L);
070 NEXT L
080 END

◆RUN

?5
?7
?9
?3
?6
        5    7    9    3    6
```

Here, five values have been entered to form the A array. The values of the array are then printed.

This next program reads ten values into the A array. The INPUT statement is used so that the user has complete control over what numbers are to be entered. The program then sorts the 10 values in increasing sequence. This program uses a method of sorting that requires several passes through the numbers of an array. Each pass interchanges pairs of numbers that are not in sequence. Each pass becomes shorter and shorter since, at the end of each pass, the largest number falls toward the bottom of the array. F is a variable that can be tested for early termination of the program. When F indicates that no interchange took place during the last pass, the program terminates since all numbers are then in sequence. Note the semicolon in the PRINT statement at line 170. This punctuation inhibits the carriage return and causes numbers to print on one line.

```
010 DIM A(10)
020 FOR J=1 TO 10
030 INPUT A(J)
040 NEXT J
050 FOR K=1 TO 9
060 LET F=0
070 FOR L=1 TO 10-K
080 IF A(L)<=A(L+1) THEN 130
090 LET T=A(L)
100 LET A(L)=A(L+1)
110 LET A(L+1)=T
120 LET F=1
130 NEXT L
140 IF F=0 THEN 160
150 NEXT K
160 FOR M=1 TO 10
170 PRINT A(M);
180 NEXT M
190 END
```

◆RUN

```
?4
?6
?8
?2
?9
?6
?4
?1
?3
?8
     1    2    3    4    4    6    6    8    8    9
```

EXERCISES

1. What is the difference between the INPUT and the READ statements?

2. Study the following program:

```
10 INPUT X
20 PRINT X,X ↑ 2
30 GO TO 10
40 END
```

What does the program do with the values that are input for X?

3. Refer to the program in Question 2. How many times will the program execute the statement at line 10?

4. Refer to the program in Question 2. How does one stop the loop that is formed by the statements at lines 10, 20, and 30? Give two ways.

5. How can a program be designed so that it tells the user what value or values are to be input?

6. Can an INPUT statement be written so it calls for more than one value? Give an example.

7. Study this next segment of a program:

```
10 FOR N = 1 TO 20
20 INPUT R
30 PRINT R, R * 3.5
40 NEXT N
```

How many times will the statements at lines 20 and 30 be executed? How many lines will the program print?

8. Study this next segment of a program:

```
10 DIM A(10)
20 INPUT A(1), A(2), A(3), A(4)
30 INPUT A(5), A(6), A(7), A(8)
40 INPUT A(9), A(10)
```

How many values will the A array receive?

9. Refer to Question 8. Rewrite the program segment so that the statements at lines 20 through 40 are replaced with a FOR/NEXT loop.

10. Write a program that accepts values of A, B, and C, via the INPUT statement, sums the values and obtains the square root of the sum. The program then prints A, B, C, and the

square root of the sum of A, B, and C. The program then repeats this procedure over and over until the STOP entry is given.

THE ON STATEMENT

The ON statement causes multiple branches to take place in a program. Consider this program:

```
10 INPUT K
20 ON K GO TO 30,50
30 – – –
40 – – –
50 – – –
60 – – –
70 END
```

The program will jump to line 30 if the value of K, the ON statement's index, is 1; it will jump to line 50 if the value of K is 2. If K is less than 1 or greater than 3, an error message will be given. Then the program will stop.

Consider the example shown below and on page 138.

```
010 INPUT K
020 ON K GO TO 30,50
030 PRINT "GOT TO 30"
040 GO TO 10
050 PRINT "GOT TO 50"
060 GO TO 10
070 END
```

```
◆RUN

?1
GOT TO 30
?2
GOT TO 50
?3

INVALID COMPUTED GOTO IN 20

◆RUN

?2
GOT TO 50
?0

INVALID COMPUTED GOTO IN 20

◆RUN

?1
GOT TO 30
?-1

INVALID COMPUTED GOTO IN 20
```

The ON statement may contain more than two line numbers. For example, these ON statements are acceptable:

          100 ON W GO TO 30, 80, 110, 50
          250 ON F GO TO 25, 300, 280

In the former example, the program will jump to line 30 if W's value is 1; to line 80 if W's value is 2, etc. In the latter example, the program will jump to line 25 if F's value is 1; to line 300 if F's value is 2, etc.

The ON statement has this form:

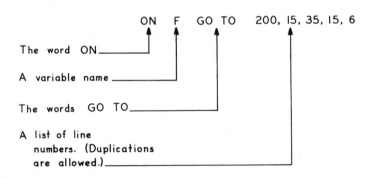

EXERCISES

1. What does the ON statement accomplish?
2. How many line numbers can you give following ON?
3. In an ON statement, what happens if the index value is out of range?
4. Study the following program:

```
10 INPUT K
20 ON K GO TO 30, 50
30 PRINT "HI"
40 GO TO 10
50 END
```

What will the program do if the value input for K is 1?
What will the program do if the value input for K is 2?
What will the program do if the value input for K is 3?

5. Study the following statement:

```
100 ON W GO TO 30, 80, 90, 85, 80, 92
```

For what values of W will the program jump to line 80?

THE GOSUB AND REM STATEMENTS

A program may jump to a subroutine. To do this, the GOSUB command is employed. The subroutine is executed. Then, when the RETURN statement in the subroutine is encountered, control returns to the main program.

In the next example, the program jumps to line 040, the starting location of a subroutine. The program continues from that point. When the RETURN statement is encountered, the program goes back to the main program—to the statement immediately following GOSUB.

```
010 DATA 4,6,2,9,5,2,2,7,6,3,0,0
015 READ A,B
020 IF A=0 GO TO 65
025 GOSUB 40
030 PRINT A;B;C
035 GO TO 15
040 IF A>B THEN 55
045 LET C=A^B
050 GO TO 60
055 LET C=B^A
060 RETURN
065 END

◆RUN

    4       6    4096
    2       9     512
    5       2      32
    2       7     128
    6       3     729
```

The statement GOSUB 40 could be given in several places of a main program. The RETURN statement will always send the program back to the statement immediately following the GOSUB that called the subroutine.

A main program may give a GOSUB to more than one subroutine. A subroutine can give a GOSUB to another subroutine. RETURNs always cause control to return to the calling program, be it a subroutine or a main program. There is more information about subroutines in the REMARK discussion that follows.

The REMARK statement is used to document a BASIC program. When a statement beginning with REM is given, the entire line on which the statement appears is considered a comment. REM may be written REM, REM:, REMARK, or any combination of characters beginning with REM. This self-documenting program explains REM:

```
010 REM THIS PROGRAM SHOWS HOW 'REMARK' STATEMENTS
020 REM MAY BE GIVEN.   THE THREE CHARACTERS 'REM'
030 REM ARE GIVEN.   WHATEVER ELSE APPEARS ON THE
040 REM LINE IS CONSIDERED A REMARK.   ONE MAY WRITE
050 REMARK OUT THE WORD 'REMARK' IF DESIRED OR
060 REM: PLACE A COLON (OR ANY OTHER CHARACTER)
070 REM# FOLLOWING 'REM'.   TO MAKE READABILITY BETTER,
080 REM
090 REM
100 REM      ONE MIGHT WANT TO SPACE OUT THE
110 REM      MESSAGES TO APPEAR LIKE THIS.
120 REM
130 REM
140 REM      REMARKS HELP DOCUMENT PROGRAMS
150 REM      SO THAT THEY CAN BE BETTER UNDERSTOOD.
160 REM
170 REM
180 REM EMPTY REMARK STATEMENTS MAY ALSO BE USED TO
190 REM HELP SEPARATE VARIOUS PARTS OF A PROGRAM.
200 REM NOTE HOW EMPTY REMS HAVE BEEN USED ABOVE TO
210 REM SEPARATE VARIOUS PARTS OF THIS PROGRAM.
220 REM
230 REM
240 REM
250 REM THE PROGRAMS THAT FOLLOW USE REM TO GIVE ADDITIONAL
260 REM INFORMATION CONCERNING HOW GOSUBS OPERATE.
270 END
```

```
010 REM      A GOSUB STATEMENT CAUSES A PROGRAM TO JUMP TO THE
020 REM      LINE THAT IS GIVEN FOLLOWING GOSUB.   THE COMMANDS
030 REM      THAT BEGIN AT THAT LINE ARE REFERRED TO AS A 'SUBROUTINE'.
040 REM      THE COMPUTER EXECUTES THE COMMANDS IN THE CALLED
050 REM      SUBROUTINE UNTIL IT ENCOUNTERS A RETURN STATEMENT.   THAT
060 REM      STATEMENT CAUSES THE COMPUTER TO GO BACK TO THE STATEMENT
070 REM      IMMEDIATELY FOLLOWING GOSUB.
080 REM
090 REM      THE PROGRAM CAN BE DIRECTED TO GO TO THE SAME
100 REM      SUBROUTINE MANY TIMES.   FOR EXAMPLE, GOSUB MAY BE
110 REM      ONE OF THE STATEMENTS IN A LOOP.
120 DATA 4,6,2,9,5,2,2,7,6,3,0,0
130 READ A,B
140 IF A=0 THEN 220
150 GOSUB 190
160 PRINT A;B;C
```

```
170 GO TO 130
180 REM      ++++++++++ SUBROUTINE BEGINS BELOW ++++++++++
190 LET C=(SQR(A) + LOG(B))/(A+B)
200 RETURN
210 REM      ++++++++++ SUBROUTINE  ENDS  ABOVE ++++++++++
220 END

+RUN

     4     6     .3791759
     2     9     .3283126
     5     2     .4184593
     2     7     .3733471
     6     3     .3942336


010 REM     IN THIS NEXT PROGRAM, THERE SHOULD BE
020 REM     A 'GO TO 130' STATEMENT FOLLOWING LINE 100.
030 LET X=4.5
040 LET Y=2.2
050 GOSUB 110
060 PRINT X;Y;Z
070 LET X=6.7
080 LET Y=9.9
090 GOSUB 110
100 PRINT X;Y;Z
110 LET Z=X+Y
120 RETURN
130 END

+RUN

   4.5   2.2   6.7
   6.7   9.9  16.6

ILLEGAL ENTRY TO SUBROUTINE
```

The main program inadvertently entered the subroutine region.
This is bad. The problem is easily resolved by inserting a GO TO
120 statement at line 105.

```
010 REM      IN THIS NEXT PROGRAM, THERE SHOULD BE
020 REM      A 'GO TO 130' STATEMENT FOLLOWING LINE 100.
030 LET X=4.5
040 LET Y=2.2
050 GOSUB 110
060 PRINT X;Y;Z
070 LET X=6.7
080 LET Y=9.9
090 GOSUB 110
100 PRINT X;Y;Z
105 GO TO 130
110 LET Z=X+Y
120 RETURN
130 END

+RUN

   4.5   2.2   6.7
   6.7   9.9  16.6
```

The next program shows a decision being made in the GOSUB area.

```
010 REM     THE SUBROUTINE IS LOCATED BETWEEN STATEMENTS
020 REM     140 AND 190, INCLUSIVE.  NOTE THE DECISION
030 REM     THAT IS BEING MADE IN THAT AREA WITH THE
040 REM     IF STATEMENT.
050 LET X=4.5
060 LET Y=2.2
070 GOSUB 140
080 PRINT X;Y;Z
090 LET X=6.7
100 LET Y=9.9
110 GOSUB 140
120 PRINT X;Y;Z
130 GO TO 200
140 REM     THE SUBROUTINE BEGINS AT THIS POINT
150 IF X>Y THEN 180
160 LET Z=X+Y
170 GO TO 190
180 LET Z=X-Y
190 RETURN
200 END

READY

◆RUN

   4.5   2.2   2.3
   6.7   9.9  16.6
```

The GOSUB statement has this form:

The REM statement has this form:

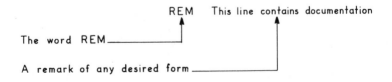

EXERCISES

1. What is a subroutine as used in BASIC?

2. What does the GOSUB statement accomplish?

3. What does the RETURN statement accomplish in a subroutine?

4. Study the following program:

```
10 INPUT A
20 IF A = 0 GO TO 80
30 GOSUB 50
40 GO TO 10
50 LET B = A ↑ 2
60 PRINT A,B
70 RETURN
80 END
```

   What is the reason that the statement at line 40 exists?
   What would happen if the statement at line 40 were not there?

5. May a subroutine give a GOSUB to another subroutine?

6. Is it possible for the program to enter a subroutine area without the programmer's intending to send it there? Explain.

7. Refer to Question 6. How can a programmer make sure that he or she will never inadvertently send a program into a subroutine area?

8. Study the program shown below and on page 146.

```
010 INPUT A,B,C,D
020 GOSUB 100
030 PRINT A,B,E
040 GOSUB 200
050 PRINT C,D,E
060 GO TO 250
100 IF A > B THEN 130
110 LET E = A - B
120 RETURN
```

```
130 LET E = A + B
140 RETURN
200 IF C > D THEN 230
210 LET E = C / D
220 RETURN
230 LET E = C * D
240 RETURN
250 END
```

When will the program add A and B?

When will the program multiply C by D?

How could you eliminate two RETURNS from this program?

How many subroutines does the program contain?

Why is there a GO TO at line 060?

In this program does E have to be initialized to zero at the beginning of the program? If not, why not?

9. What does the REMARK line in a BASIC program accomplish?

10. What are the various ways that you might spell REMARK? Explain.

11. Study this program:

```
10 REM LET A = 5
20 REM LET B = 6
30 REM PRINT A,B,A + B
40 REM END
50 END
```

What does the program print?

12. Would you agree that most complex programs should use many REMARK lines?

ALPHANUMERIC PROCESSING

Words and phrases, as well as numbers, can be assigned to variable names. Example:

```
010 LET A$="THE DATA IS"
020 LET B$="INCORRECT"
030 PRINT A$,B$
040 PRINT A$;B$
050 PRINT B$,A$
060 PRINT B$;A$
070 END

◆RUN


THE DATA IS    INCORRECT
THE DATA ISINCORRECT
INCORRECT      THE DATA IS
INCORRECTTHE DATA IS
```

The words and phrases are given within quotes. Blanks within quotes are significant. Compare this next program with the one above. Note how a blank is given to A$ to separate IS and INCORRECT.

```
010 LET A$="THE DATA IS "
020 LET B$="INCORRECT"
030 PRINT A$,B$
040 PRINT A$;B$
050 PRINT B$,A$
060 PRINT B$;A$
070 END

◆RUN

THE DATA IS      INCORRECT
THE DATA IS INCORRECT
INCORRECT       THE DATA IS
INCORRECTTHE DATA IS
```

Another example:

```
010 LET A$="THE DATA IS "
020 LET B$=" INCORRECT "
030 PRINT A$,B$
040 PRINT A$;B$
050 PRINT B$,A$
060 PRINT B$;A$
070 END

◆RUN

THE DATA IS      INCORRECT
THE DATA IS  INCORRECT
 INCORRECT       THE DATA IS
 INCORRECT THE DATA IS
```

Data that consist of letters of the alphabet, digits, and special symbols are called alphanumeric data. Alphanumeric data can be read from DATA statements. Observe how values can be assigned to A\$ and B\$. Names used to hold alphanumeric values must include an appended \$ (dollar sign).

```
010 DATA THE DATA IS,INCORRECT
020 READ A$,B$
030 PRINT A$;B$
040 END

◆RUN

THE DATA ISINCORRECT
```

Names such as A$, T$, F3$, Z9$, etc., are acceptable for holding alphanumeric values. The rules for forming these names are the same as the rules for forming ordinary variable names except that a dollar sign ($) must be appended to the names. You can assign words, symbols, phrases, even entire sentences to alphanumeric variable names. In most BASIC systems at least 60 characters can be assigned to alphanumeric names.

If blanks are needed in alphanumeric values, it is not sufficient to include blanks between values in the DATA statement. Example:

```
010 DATA THE DATA IS, INCORRECT
020 READ A$,B$
030 PRINT A$;B$
040 END

◆RUN

THE DATA ISINCORRECT
```

When alphanumeric values are enclosed in quotes, however, blanks can be included in those values if required.

```
010 DATA "THE DATA IS"," INCORRECT"
020 READ A$,B$
030 PRINT A$;B$
040 END

◆RUN

THE DATA IS INCORRECT
```

If alphanumeric values do not include blanks, digits, or special signs, quotes are not needed.

Suppose, for example, we wish to assign a date to B$. This is the wrong way to do it:

```
010 DATA THE DATE TODAY IS,MARCH 21,1976
020 READ A$,B$
030 PRINT A$;B$
040 END

◆RUN

THE DATE TODAY ISMARCH 21
```

The comma in the date causes the wrong value to be assigned to B$. An attempt to get a better read is shown below:

```
010 DATA THE DATE TODAY IS,MARCH 21,1976
020 READ A$,B$,X
030 PRINT A$;B$;X
040 END

◆RUN

THE DATE TODAY ISMARCH 21 1976
```

The numeric part of the date is assigned to X. But now, the comma in the date has disappeared. It can be materialized this way: (Note the comma given within quotes on line 030.)

```
010 DATA THE DATE TODAY IS,MARCH 21,1976
020 READ A$,B$,X
030 PRINT A$;B$;",";X
040 END

◆RUN

THE DATE TODAY ISMARCH 21, 1976
```

A much cleaner way to assign the date to B$ is to enclose it within quotes:

```
010 DATA THE DATE TODAY IS," MARCH 21,1979"
020 READ A$,B$
030 PRINT A$;B$
040 END

◆RUN

THE DATE TODAY IS MARCH 21,1979
```

Alphanumeric values can be entered via the INPUT statement:

```
010 PRINT "PLEASE TYPE IN DATE"
020 INPUT D$
030 PRINT D$
040 END

◆RUN

PLEASE TYPE IN DATE
?MARCH 21,1979
ILLEGAL INPUT. RETYPE?"MARCH 21, 1979"
MARCH 21, 1979
```

Observe that here, too, quotes are needed around alphanumeric values that include digits, blanks, or special signs. The program objected to the INPUT entry because the comma in the date made it appear that two values were being entered where the program expected only one.

This next program attempts to read ten alphanumeric values into the A$ array.

```
010 DIM A$(10)
020 DATA ABC,DEF,GHI,JKL,MNO,PQR,STU
030 DATA VWX,YZ1,234
040 FOR J=1 TO 10
050 READ A$(J)
060 NEXT J
070 FOR K=1 TO 10
080 PRINT A$(K)
090 NEXT K
100 END

◆RUN

OUT OF DATA IN  50
```

The attempt fails because the numeric value 234 is not enclosed within quotes. Contrast the above program with this next one.

```
010 DIM A$(10)
020 DATA ABC,DEF,GHI,JKL,MNO,PQR,STU
030 DATA VWX,YZ1,"234"
040 FOR J=1 TO 10
050 READ A$(J)
060 NEXT J
070 FOR K=1 TO 10
080 PRINT A$(K)
090 NEXT K
100 END

◆RUN

ABC
DEF
GHI
JKL
MNO
PQR
STU
VWX
YZ1
234
```

We know that A$$_{10}$ contains a pure number, but BASIC does not permit a value assigned to a name having a dollar sign to be used in calculations. Note line 065.

```
010 DIM A$(10)
020 DATA ABC,DEF,GHI,JKL,MNO,PQR,STU
030 DATA VWX,YZ1,"234"
040 FOR J=1 TO 10
050 READ A$(J)
060 NEXT J
065 LET X=A$(10)+5
070 FOR K=1 TO 10
080 PRINT A$(K)
090 NEXT K
100 END


◆RUN
065 LET X=A$(10)+5
              ^
STATEMENT ERROR
```

The computer system tells us that the statement at line 065 is illegal.

This next program establishes two arrays—C$, containing five catalog numbers, and P, containing five corresponding prices. The program inputs V$, a catalog number; finds the catalog number in the C$ array; then prints the catalog number and its corresponding price.

```
010 DIM C$(5),P(5)
020 DATA "156-X",35,"162-Z",87,"247◆L",33
030 DATA "976◆E",34,"76◆◆8L",21
040 FOR N=1 TO 5
050 READ C$(N),P(N)
060 NEXT N
070 INPUT V$
080 IF V$="STOP" THEN 160
090 FOR W=1 TO 5
100 IF C$(W)=V$ THEN 140
110 NEXT W
120 PRINT "CAT ";V$;" NOT FOUND"
130 GO TO 70
140 PRINT C$(W);P(W)
150 GO TO 70
160 END

◆RUN
```

```
?"162-Z"
162-Z    87
?"76♦♦8L"
76♦♦8L    21
?"233-F"
CAT 233-F NOT FOUND
?"156-X"
156-X    35
?STOP
```

The program prints an error message whenever a desired catalog number is not found.

Using the interchange method of sorting (the same as used for sorting numeric values), a program can sequence alphanumeric values. Here is a program that accomplishes the task:

```
010 DIM A$(10)
020 DATA BBB,CAF,GGH,QWE,"23DD","UU3",AAB,AAA,"AA3"
030 DATA "3AA"
040 FOR W=1 TO 10
050 READ A$(W)
060 NEXT W
070 FOR I=1 TO 9
075 LET F=0
080 FOR J=1 TO 10-I
090 IF A$(J)<=A$(J+1) THEN 130
100 LET T$=A$(J)
110 LET A$(J)=A$(J+1)
120 LET A$(J+1)=T$
125 LET F=1
130 NEXT J
135 IF F=0 THEN 150
140 NEXT I
150 FOR K=1 TO 10
160 PRINT A$(K)
170 NEXT K
180 END

♦RUN

23DD
3AA
AA3
AAA
AAB
BBB
CAF
GGH
QWE
UU3
```

EXERCISES

1. Give a statement that assigns the word TRUMBULL to Q$.
2. Study the next program:

```
10 LET A$ = "THE DATA"
20 LET B$ = "IS CORRECT"
30 PRINT A$; B$
40 END
```

What will the program print? Will there be a blank between the words DATA and IS?

3. What are the rules for inventing a name to which an alphanumeric value is to be assigned?

4. Can alphanumeric values be read from a DATA statement? Give an example of a DATA statement containing the word AIRLINE. Give the READ statement for this value to be assigned to a variable named D$.

5. Can alphanumeric values be input from the terminal using the INPUT statement? When would quotes be given in the value that is being input?

6. Write a program that assigns your name to A$. Then have the program print A$ five times. Use a FOR/NEXT loop.

RANDOM NUMBERS

The computer system can be requested to give random numbers, that is, numbers that appear to be given as if they were being drawn out of a box containing all possible numbers between 0 and 1. Random numbers are used in programs involving statistical analysis, games, and simulations. Random numbers given by a computer may be any numbers from 0 to 1 (zero is included as a possibility, but 1 is not.) Example:

```
010 FOR I=1 TO 5
020 PRINT RND (0)
030 NEXT I
040 END

◆RUN

    .7886751
    .5277669
    .8706056
    .0968034
    .2763165
```

The built-in routine that gives random numbers is RND. When the argument given to RND is zero, the computer gives the *same* list of random numbers whenever the program is run. The list of numbers contains several billion numbers, a virtually endless supply. If a user needs another *repeatable* list of random numbers, he or she can give as RND's argument any positive number greater than zero. Example:

```
010 FOR I = 1 TO 5
020 PRINT RND (45)
030 NEXT I
040 END

◆RUN

     .1402376
     .8793294
     .2221681
     .4483659
      .627879
```

Note the argument, 45, at line 020. That argument, when used, *always* gives a series of random numbers beginning with the ones shown above. If the argument had been 46, or 23, or 91, etc., a *different* repeatable set of random numbers would have been given.

The next program shows that a program can be run more than once giving the same set of random numbers each time:

```
010 INPUT N
020 FOR I = 1 TO 5
030 PRINT RND (N)
040 NEXT I
050 GO TO 10
060 END

◆RUN

?83
     .1128939
     .3519857
     .1948244
     .9210222
     .6005353
?STOP

  ◆RUN

  ?22
      .1324251
      .8715169
      .2143556
      .4405534
      .6200665
  ?STOP
```

```
◆RUN

?83
        .1128939
        .3519857
        .1948244
        .9210222
        .6005353
?STOP


◆RUN

?22
        .1324251
        .8715169
        .2143556
        .4405534
        .6200665
?STOP
```

When RND's argument is a negative number—any negative number—the program gives unpredictable, unrepeatable numbers. Example:

```
010 FOR K=1 TO 5
020 PRINT RND(-1)
030 NEXT K
040 END

◆RUN

        .0855501
        .8246419
        .1674806
        .3936784
        .5731915


◆RUN

        .5191439
        .7582356
        .6010744
        .3272722
        .0067853
```

Observe that there is no apparent relationship between the first run and the second.

The average of many random numbers should be about 0.5. This first program gives the average of 100 numbers.

```
010 LET S = 0
020 FOR I = 1 TO 100
030 LET D = RND (-1)
040 LET S = S + D
050 NEXT I
060 PRINT S / 100
070 END

◆RUN

    .5464214
```

The average is closer to 0.5 when 1000 numbers are averaged.

```
010 LET S = 0
020 FOR I = 1 TO 1000
030 LET D = RND (-1)
040 LET S = S + D
050 NEXT I
060 PRINT S / 1000
070 END

◆RUN

    .4973284
```

Random numbers that are less than 1 can be converted to integers within any desired range. In the program that follows, G is an integer number that lies between 14 and 21, inclusive.

```
010 FOR J = 1 TO 10
020 LET F = RND(-1)
030 LET G=INT(F◆8)+14
040 PRINT G;
050 NEXT J
060 END

◆RUN

    14    15    14    20    17    15    21    15    21    19
```

In the statement at line 030, the number 8 tells how many values there are in the series, and 14 tells what is the first number of the series. Each number in the series has an equal opportunity to appear.

This next program obtains 1000 random numbers. Each number is examined to determine whether it begins with 0, 1, 2, 3, etc. The count of how many numbers begin with 0, 1, 2, 3, etc. is stored in array A. Below is a listing that shows the program and its output.

```
010 DIM X(10)
020 FOR J=1 TO 1000
030 LET Q=RND(-1)
040 LET R=INT(Q*10)+1
050 LET X(R)=X(R)+1
060 NEXT J
070 FOR K=1 TO 10
080 PRINT K-1;
090 NEXT K
100 FOR K=1 TO 10
110 PRINT X(K);
120 NEXT K
130 END

◆RUN

    0     1     2     3     4     5     6     7   8     9    97   128
   94   107   108   103   104    83    86    90
```

The printout is confusing because of the semicolon at line 080. We need two separate lines instead of one continuous line. An extra PRINT statement between the two existing PRINT statements causes two separate lines to be printed instead of a single continuous one. In the next program, note the PRINT statement at line 095.

```
010 DIM X(10)
020 FOR J=1 TO 1000
030 LET Q=RND(-1)
040 LET R=INT(Q*10)+1
050 LET X(R)=X(R)+1
060 NEXT J
070 FOR K=1 TO 10
080 PRINT K-1;
090 NEXT K
095 PRINT
100 FOR K=1 TO 10
110 PRINT X(K);
120 NEXT K
130 END

◆RUN

    0     1     2     3     4     5     6     7     8     9
  109   106    95    96    95    89    88    94   130    98
```

◆RUN

0	1	2	3	4	5	6	7	8	9
93	132	95	113	104	95	96	94	87	91

The program shows that 109 numbers begin with 0, 106 with 1, 95 with 2, etc. Two runs of the program were made; the output is reproduced above. On a purely random basis, one would expect about 100 numbers in each category. The same program has run using 10,000 numbers instead of only 1000; the output is reproduced below.

```
010 DIM X(10)
020 FOR J=1 TO 10000
030 LET Q=RND(-1)
040 LET R=INT(Q*10)+1
050 LET X(R)=X(R)+1
060 NEXT J
070 FOR K=1 TO 10
080 PRINT K-1;
090 NEXT K
095 PRINT
100 FOR K=1 TO 10
110 PRINT X(K);
120 NEXT K
130 END
```

◆RUN

0	1	2	3	4	5	6	7	8	9
956	1013	980	1040	1034	954	1040	993	1045	945

On a purely random basis, one would expect about 1000 numbers in each category.

This final example shows how the path of a particle moving randomly can be simulated. In the program, the particle begins at the point X = 0, Y = 0, then moves north, south, east, and west in a series of 100 moves. The final resting place is printed out. The program simulates ten experiments. At the end of the first experiment, the final resting point is X = -11, Y = 11; the second is X = -5, Y = -3; etc.

```
10 FOR J=1 TO 10
15 LET X=0
20 LET Y=0
25 FOR K=1 TO 100
30 LET R=RND(-1)
35 LET T=INT(R*4)+1
```

```
40 ON T GO TO 45,55,65,75
45 LET X=X+1
50 GO TO 80
55 LET X=X-1
60 GO TO 80
65 LET Y=Y+1
70 GO TO 80
75 LET Y=Y-1
80 NEXT K
85 PRINT X;Y
90 NEXT J
95 END
```

◆RUN

```
-11      11
 -5      -3
-14       2
  7       3
-11       3
  2       0
-13       5
  5       3
 -6       4
 -4      -2
```

EXERCISES

1. What is a random number? What are random numbers used for?

2. What is the largest random number that BASIC gives? The smallest?

3. What is the name of the built-in routine that gives random numbers?

4. Give three kinds of arguments that may be given to the RND function. What does each argument type do?

5. If you ask BASIC to give you 1000 random numbers, what is the approximate average value of those numbers? That is, if all 1000 numbers were summed, and that sum were divided by 1000, what would be the most likely result?

6. What equation do you give when you wish to convert a series of random numbers to a series of integers within some given range?

7. Study this program:

```
10 LET W = RND (-1)
20 PRINT W
30 END
```

What can you predict about the random number that the program will give?

8. Study this program:

```
010 LET N = RND (-1)
020 LET P = RND (-1)
030 IF N > P THEN 70
040 IF N = P THEN 90
050 PRINT "A"
060 GO TO 100
070 PRINT "B"
080 GO TO 100
090 PRINT "C"
100 END
```

What can you predict about whether the program will print A, B, or C?

9. Study this program:

```
10 LET G = RND(0)
20 LET H = INT (G*5) + 3
30 PRINT H
40 END
```

If G's value is .7886751, what value will the computer print?

10. Study this program:

```
10 LET D = RND (-1)
20 PRINT D
30 END
```

Is it possible for D's value to be zero? Is it possible for D's value to be 1?

MATRIX COMMANDS

In BASIC, two-dimensional arrays can be defined and processed. Example:

    10 DIM A(3,4)

An area named A having dimensions of 3 rows by 4 columns is being defined. It looks like this:

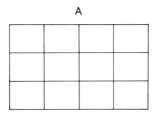

In the DIM statement, the meanings of the various parts are these:

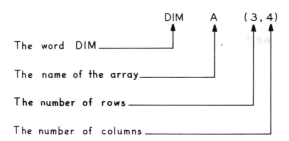

Values can be read into a two-dimensional array this way:

```
10 DIM A(3,4)
20 DATA 6, 6, 5, 8, 2, 9, 7, 7, 6, 3, 2, 4
30 FOR J = 1 TO 3
40 FOR K = 1 TO 4
50 READ A(J,K)
60 NEXT K
70 NEXT J
      .
      .
      .
```

There are two loops, one inside the other. The row variable, J, remains constant while the column variable, K, cycles from 1 through 4. Then the row variable changes to 2 while the column variable cycles from 1 through 4 again, etc. The values are read into the array this way:

6	6	5	8
2	9	7	7
6	3	2	4

When numbers are loaded into a two-dimensional array, it is said that a matrix exists. Work can be done with matrices, as we shall see later. The BASIC language gives the user twelve commands that can be used with matrices. In a matrix, subscripts tell what row and what column is being accessed. For example, if an array's name is A and the subscripts are 3 and 4, the element of the array A being processed is the one where Row 3 and Column 4 intersect. The leftmost subscript is always the row subscript, and the rightmost is always the column subscript.

MAT READ AND MAT PRINT

The MAT READ command causes *all* values needed to fill an array to be read from DATA statement(s) located in a program. The MAT PRINT command causes those values to be printed. Example:

```
010 DATA 3,5,7,8,2,9,5,6,4
020 DATA 7,8,3,5,6,7,8,2,1
030 DATA 5,7,8,2,0,7,5
040 DIM A(5,5)
050 MAT READ A
060 MAT PRINT A
070 END
```

◆RUN

3	5	7	8	2
9	5	6	4	7
8	3	5	6	7
8	2	1	5	7
8	2	0	7	5

The values are read into the A array. That array consists of five columns and five rows. The entire array is then printed. Observe that when the array is loaded from DATA statements, the first row is filled first, then the second row, then the third, etc. Observe, also, that, when dealing with matrices, the letters MAT are placed ahead of the words READ and PRINT.

The values in the array can be printed closer together by placing a semicolon following the array name in the PRINT statement. (See the example below.)

```
010 DATA 3,5,7,8,2,9,5,6,4
020 DATA 7,8,3,5,6,7,8,2,1
030 DATA 5,7,8,2,0,7,5
040 DIM A(5,5)
050 MAT READ A
060 MAT PRINT A;
070 END
```

◆RUN

3	5	7	8	2
9	5	6	4	7
8	3	5	6	7
8	2	1	5	7
8	2	0	7	5

 Arrays can be defined having up to 99 rows and 99 columns. When printing large arrays, each row of the array will require more than one printed line on the terminal. In this chapter, we'll discuss small arrays—those that require only one printed line per row. The MAT READ command can redefine the size of an array to be read. The corresponding PRINT statement remembers that redefinition. Here is an example:

```
010 DATA 3,5,7,8,2,9,5,6,4
020 DATA 7,8,3,5,6,7,8,2,1
030 DATA 5,7,8,2,0,7,5
040 DIM A(5,5)
050 MAT READ A (3,4)
060 MAT PRINT A;
070 END

◆RUN


 3       5       7       8

 2       9       5       6

 4       7       8       3
```

As you've seen, if the READ statement does not give the dimensions of an array, the array's DIM statement is used to give dimension information.

 The next example shows that the data values used in the previous program can be read into a 6 by 4 array:

```
010 DATA 3,5,7,8,2,9,5,6,4
020 DATA 7,8,3,5,6,7,8,2,1
030 DATA 5,7,8,2,0,7,5
040 DIM A(6,4)
050 MAT READ A
060 MAT PRINT A;
070 END

◆RUN
 3       5       7       8

 2       9       5       6

 4       7       8       3

 5       6       7       8

 2       1       5       7

 8       2       0       7
```

or into a 4 by 6 array:

```
010 DATA 3,5,7,8,2,9,5,6,4
020 DATA 7,8,3,5,6,7,8,2,1
030 DATA 5,7,8,2,0,7,5
040 DIM A(4,6)
050 MAT READ A
060 MAT PRINT A;
070 END

◆RUN
```

3	5	7	8	2	9
5	6	4	7	8	3
5	6	7	8	2	1
5	7	8	2	0	7

Observe that there must be enough values in one or more DATA statements to satisfy the MAT READ command; otherwise the MAT READ command will fail. Note this example:

```
010 DATA 3,5,7,8,2,9,5,6,4,7,8,2
020 DATA 3,9,6,9,4,5,1,2,0,3,9,2,3
030 DIM A(6,6)
040 MAT READ A
050 MAT PRINT A;
060 END

◆RUN

OUT OF DATA IN   40
```

Observe that more than one array can be read and printed at one time, as shown below and on the following page.

```
010 DATA 3,5,7,8,2,9,5,6,4,7,8,2
020 DATA 3,9,6,9,4,5,1,2,0
030 DIM A(3,3),B(2,4),C(2,2)
040 MAT READ A,B,C
050 MAT PRINT A;B;C;
060 END

◆RUN
```

```
3       5       7

8       2       9

5       6       4


7       8       2       3

9       6       9       4


5       1

2       0
```

The MAT INPUT statement can be used in place of the MAT READ statement. For example:

```
010 DIM A(4,4)
020 MAT INPUT A
030 MAT PRINT A;
040 END

◆RUN

?1,2,3,4,5,6,7,8,1,2,3,4,5,6,7,8
```

```
1       2       3       4

5       6       7       8

1       2       3       4

5       6       7       8
```

The computer system types a question mark. The user then supplies the values needed by the array. If more than enough values are given, the system ignores the extra values. Example:

```
010 DIM A(4,4)
020 MAT INPUT A
030 MAT PRINT A;
040 END

◆RUN
```

```
?1,2,3,4,5,6,7,8,2,3,3,4,5,6,7,8,1,2,3,4
     1     2     3     4

     5     6     7     8

     2     3     3     4

     5     6     7     8
```

If fewer values are given than what the array calls for, the remainder of the array is filled with zeroes. Example:

```
010 DIM A(4,4)
020 MAT INPUT A
030 MAT PRINT A;
040 END

♦RUN


?1,2,3,4,5,6,7,8
        1     2     3     4

        5     6     7     8

        0     0     0     0

        0     0     0     0
```

The MAT INPUT statement can be used to redimension a matrix just as the MAT READ statement can be used to do this. Example:

```
010 DIM A(4,4)
020 MAT INPUT A(2,2)
030 MAT PRINT A;
040 END

♦RUN

?1,2,3,4
        1     2

        3     4
```

A one-dimensional array can be read and printed as shown by the example that follows:

```
010 DIM A(10)
020 DATA 4,6,3,7,8,1,2,9,5,9
030 MAT READ A
040 MAT PRINT A;
050 END

◆RUN

      4

      6

      3

      7

      8

      1

      2

      9

      5

      9
```

ADDITION

Matrices may be added. This next example shows how matrices A and B can be added and the result assigned to matrix C.

```
010 DATA 2,6,7,3,4,5,9,6,5,3
020 DATA 2,4,7,8,5,1,2,0,5,3
030 DATA 3,2,5,7,4,5,8,9,1,2
040 DATA 3,4
050 DIM A(4,4),B(4,4),C(4,4)
060 MAT READ A,B
070 MAT C=A+B
080 MAT PRINT A;B;C;
090 END

◆RUN
```

2	6	7	3
4	5	9	6
5	3	2	4
7	8	5	1

2	0	5	3
3	2	5	7
4	5	8	9
1	2	3	4

4	6	12	6
7	7	14	13
9	8	10	13
8	10	8	5

Observe that every element of the A matrix is added to the corresponding element of the B matrix, and the result is assigned to the corresponding element of the C matrix.

SUBTRACTION

Matrices may be subtracted. In the next example, every element of the B matrix is subtracted from every element of the A matrix, and the result is assigned to the corresponding element of the C matrix.

```
010 DATA 2,6,7,3,4,5,9,6,5,3
020 DATA 2,4,7,8,5,1,2,0,5,3
030 DATA 3,2,5,7,4,5,8,9,1,2
040 DATA 3,4
050 DIM A(4,4),B(4,4),C(4,4)
060 MAT READ A,B
070 MAT C=A-B
080 MAT PRINT A;B;C;
090 END
```

◆RUN

2	6	7	3
4	5	9	6
5	3	2	4
7	8	5	1

2	0	5	3
3	2	5	7
4	5	8	9
1	2	3	4

0	6	2	0
1	3	4	-1
1	-2	-6	-5
6	6	2	-3

MULTIPLICATION

Matrices can be multiplied. The term *multiplication* has a mathematical meaning that we won't go into here. If you are not a mathematician but want to understand what the next example means, observe that:

$$2 \times 2 + 6 \times 3 + 7 \times 4 + 3 \times 1 = 53;$$
$$2 \times 0 + 6 \times 2 + 7 \times 5 + 3 \times 2 = 53;$$
$$2 \times 5 + 6 \times 5 + 7 \times 8 + 3 \times 3 = 105;$$
$$2 \times 3 + 6 \times 7 + 7 \times 9 + 3 \times 4 = 123;$$
$$4 \times 2 + 5 \times 3 + 9 \times 4 + 6 \times 1 = 65;$$
$$4 \times 0 + 5 \times 2 + 9 \times 5 + 6 \times 2 = 67; \text{etc.}$$

In each product, the first number is taken from the A matrix and the second from the B matrix. Study the numbers carefully. You will see that the products come from the rows of the A matrix and the columns of the B matrix. The first row of the A matrix is processed against the first column of the B matrix. Then the first row of the A matrix is processed against the second column of the B matrix, etc. The results are stored in $C_{1,1}$, $C_{1,2}$, etc. until the last result is obtained and stored in $C_{4,4}$.

```
010 DATA 2,6,7,3,4,5,9,6,5,3
020 DATA 2,4,7,8,5,1,2,0,5,3
030 DATA 3,2,5,7,4,5,8,9,1,2
040 DATA 3,4
050 DIM A(4,4),B(4,4),C(4,4)
060 MAT READ A,B
070 MAT C=A◆B
080 MAT PRINT A;B;C;
090 END
```

◆RUN

```
    2      6      7      3

    4      5      9      6

    5      3      2      4

    7      8      5      1


    2      0      5      3

    3      2      5      7

    4      5      8      9

    1      2      3      4


   53     53    105    123

   65     67    135    152

   31     24     68     70

   59     43    118    126
```

INVERSION

A matrix may be inverted. The term *inversion* has a mathematical meaning as does *multiplication*. In the example shown below and on the following page, the A matrix is inverted.

```
010 DATA 2,6,7,3,4,5,9,6,5
020 DIM A(3,3),B(3,3)
030 MAT READ A
040 MAT B=INV(A)
050 MAT PRINT A;B;
060 END
```

```
◆RUN
```

```
        2       6       7

        3       4       5

        9       6       5



    -.2941176       .3529412       .0588235

     .8823529      -1.558824       .3235294

    -.5294118       1.235294      -.2941176
```

Matrices may be inverted to find roots of equations. The next two
programs are self-explanatory.

```
010 REM      THIS PROGRAM FINDS THE ROOTS OF THE TWO EQUATIONS
020 REM           X +  Y =  5
030 REM          3X + 4Y = 18
040 REM      THE ARRAY A CONSISTS OF THE VALUES 1,1,3,4
050 REM      AND THE ARRAY B CONSISTS OF THE VALUES 5,18
060 REM      THE ARRAY I IS THE INVERTED ARRAY, AND THE
070 REM      ARRAY X GIVES THE RESULTS.
080 REM      THE RELATIONSHIP X = A (INVERSE) TIMES B
090 REM      IS USED TO OBTAIN THE DESIRED ROOTS STORED IN
100 REM      THE ARRAY X.
110 DIM A(2,2)
120 DIM B(2)
130 DIM I(2,2)
140 DIM X(2)
150 DATA 1,1,3,4
160 DATA 5,18
170 MAT READ A
180 MAT READ B
190 MAT I=INV(A)
200 MAT X=I◆B
210 MAT PRINT A;B;I;X;
220 END

◆RUN


        1       1

        3       4



    5

18
```

```
 4     -1

-3      1


 2

 3
```

The roots of the two equations are X = 2 and Y = 3.

```
010 REM        THIS PROGRAM COMPUTES THE ROOTS OF
020 REM            A +  B +  C + D = 10
030 REM           2A +  B +  C + D = 11
040 REM            A + 2B +  C + D = 12
050 REM            A +  B + 2C + D = 13
060 DIM A(4,4)
070 DIM B(4)
080 DIM I(4,4)
090 DIM X(4)
100 DATA 1,1,1,1,2,1,1,1,1,2,1,1,1,1,2,1
110 DATA 10,11,12,13
120 MAT READ A
130 MAT READ B
140 MAT I=INV(A)
150 MAT X=I◆B
160 MAT PRINT A;B;I;X;
170 END

◆RUN


     1      1      1      1

     2      1      1      1

     1      2      1      1

     1      1      2      1


    10

    11

    12

    13
```

```
-1        1        0        0

-1        0        1        0

-1        0        0        1

 4       -1       -1       -1



 1

 2

 3

 4
```

The roots of the equations are A = 1, B = 2, C = 3, and D = 4.

TRANSPOSITION

A matrix can be transposed.   To see what is meant by the term
transpose, study the example below:

```
010 DATA 2,6,7,3,4,5,9,6,5
020 DIM A(3,3),B(3,3)
030 MAT READ A
040 MAT B=TRN(A)
050 MAT PRINT A;B;
060 END

◆RUN

        2        6        7

        3        4        5

        9        6        5


        2        3        9

        6        4        6

        7        5        5
```

Note that the top row of values becomes the leftmost column, the second row becomes the second column, etc.

MULTIPLICATION BY CONSTANT

Every element in a matrix may be multiplied by a constant. The constant may be a number, a name, or an expression. Example:

```
010 DATA 2,6,7,3,4,5,9,6,5
020 DIM A(3,3),B(3,3)
030 MAT READ A
040 MAT B=(5)*A
050 MAT PRINT A;B;
060 END

*RUN
```

```
   2      6      7

   3      4      5

   9      6      5



  10     30     35

  15     20     25

  45     30     25
```

Every element in the array was multiplied by 5. The multiplier could have been represented by a name such as K or N. A multiplier can also be an expression. The following example shows a multiplier of (10/2) * 3.

```
010 DATA 2,6,7,3,4,5,9,6,5
020 DIM A(3,3),B(3,3)
030 MAT READ A
040 MAT B=A*((10/2)*3)
050 MAT PRINT A;B;
060 END

*RUN
```

```
    2        6        7

    3        4        5

    9        6        5


   30       90      105

   45       60       75

  135       90       75
```

CONSTANT ONE

An array can be set to all 1s by giving the command:

10 MAT A = CON

CONSTANT ZERO

An array can be set to all zeroes by giving the command:

20 MAT B = ZER

IDENTITY MATRIX

An identity matrix (ones in the diagonal, zeroes elsewhere) can be
established by using the command:

30 MAT C = IDN

The three matrix commands mentioned above are illustrated
in this next example:

```
005 DIM A(5,5),B(5,4),C(4,4)
010 MAT A=CON
020 MAT B=ZER
030 MAT C=IDN
040 MAT PRINT A;B;C
050 END

◆RUN
```

```
1       1       1       1       1

1       1       1       1       1

1       1       1       1       1

1       1       1       1       1

1       1       1       1       1


0       0       0       0

0       0       0       0

0       0       0       0

0       0       0       0

0       0       0       0


1       0       0       0

0       1       0       0

0       0       1       0

0       0       0       1
```

The CON, ZER, and IDN matrix commands can redimension the effected matrix as shown below and on the next page.

```
005 DIM A(5,5),B(5,4),C(4,4)
010 MAT A=CON(3,3)
020 MAT B=ZER(3,3)
030 MAT C=IDN(3,3)
040 MAT PRINT A;B;C;
050 END

◆RUN
```

```
1       1       1

1       1       1

1       1       1
```

```
            0        0        0

            0        0        0

            0        0        0


            1        0        0

            0        1        0

            0        0        1
```

In the previous chapter you saw that MAT READ and MAT INPUT
can also redimension matrices. MAT PRINT remembers redimen-
sioned matrices but does not redimension them. The next example
also shows three matrices using CON, ZER, and IDN being re-
dimensioned. The redimensioning information is entered from a
terminal's keyboard.

```
003 INPUT I,J,K,L,M,N
005 DIM A(5,5),B(5,4),C(4,4)
010 MAT A=CON(I,J)
020 MAT B=ZER(K,L)
030 MAT C=IDN(M,N)
040 MAT PRINT A;B;C;
050 END

◆RUN

?4,3,3,2,3,3
            1        1        1

            1        1        1

            1        1        1

            1        1        1


            0        0

            0        0

            0        0
```

```
1       0       0

0       1       0

0       0       1
```

EXERCISES

1. Tell what a two-dimensional array is. What's the difference between an array and a matrix?

2. Draw the array that corresponds with this DIM statement:

    10 DIM B(4,3)

3. Give the DIM statement that corresponds with this array:

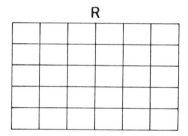

R

4. Show what the matrix named H looks like after this program has been executed:

    ```
    10 DIM H(2,3)
    20 DATA 9,4,5,6,8,3
    30 FOR L = 1 TO 2
    40 FOR M = 1 TO 3
    50 READ (L,M)
    60 NEXT M
    70 NEXT L
        .
        .
        .
    ```

5. Show what the matrix named H looks like after this program has been executed:

```
10 DIM H(2,3)
20 DATA 9,4,5,6,8,3
30 FOR L = 1 TO 3
40 FOR M = 1 TO 2
50 READ H (M,L)
60 NEXT M
70 NEXT L
        .
        .
        .
        .
```

6. Show what the matrix named H looks like after this program has been executed:

```
10 DIM H(2,3)
20 DATA 9,4,5,6,8,3
30 MAT READ H
        .
        .
        .
        .
```

7. Show what the matrix named C looks like after this program has been executed:

```
10 DATA 3,8,9,4,7,6,3,4
20 DATA 7,9,4,8,7,5,3,6
30 DIM C(4,4)
40 MAT READ C(3,2)
50 MAT PRINT C;
60 END
```

8. Study this next program. Will it execute properly? Explain.

```
10 DATA 9,4,8,7,3,6,0,4
20 DATA 3,7,4,8,4,3,7,6
30 DIM A(4,5)
```

40 MAT READ A

50 MAT PRINT A

60 END

9. Tell how MAT READ differs from MAT INPUT.

10. Show the output that would be given by this program:

    10 DIM D(5)

    20 DATA 7,4,9,3,2

    30 MAT READ D

    40 MAT PRINT D;

    50 END

11. Write a program that creates this array and then prints it. The name of the array is T.

I	0	0	0	0
0	I	0	0	0
0	0	I	0	0
0	0	0	I	0
0	0	0	0	I

12. Write a program that creates the array shown below. Then have the program print the array. The array's name is W.

I	I	I	I	I
I	0	0	0	I
I	0	0	0	I
I	0	0	0	I
I	I	I	I	I

13. Tell what is meant by the statement that matrices can be added.

14. Study this program. Show what the C matrix will contain after the program executes.

```
10 DIM A(3,3), B(3,3), C(3,3)
20 DATA 4,7,6,3,9,9,5,1,9
30 DATA 7,4,5,8,2,1,6,3,4
40 MAT READ A,B
50 MAT C = A - B
60 MAT PRINT C
70 END
```

15. Does the term *matrix multiplication* have a special mathematical meaning?

16. What matrix type would mathematicians use to compute roots of equations?

17. Study this matrix:

4	8	3
4	6	9
6	8	3

Show what it would look like if it were transposed.

18. Study the D matrix shown below:

7	9	6
6	5	3
4	0	8

What would the E matrix look like if this matrix command were performed:

MAT E = (3) * D

19. Show what this F array would look like if the command

    MAT F = CON

    were employed:

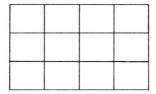

20. Refer to Question 19. What would the matrix look like if the command

    MAT F = ZER

    were employed?

21. Refer to Question 19. What would the matrix look like if the command

    MAT F = IDN

    were employed?

22. What are the five types of matrix commands that can re-dimension a matrix?

23. Write a program that creates and prints the matrix shown below. The name of the matrix is D.

17	24	1	8	15
23	5	7	14	16
4	6	13	20	22
10	12	19	21	3
11	18	25	2	9

Note that this is a magic square—all rows, columns, and diagonals have values that total 65.

24. Write a program that creates and prints the matrix shown below. The name of the matrix is A$.

A	B	C	D	E
F	G	H	J	K
L	M	N	O	P
Q	R	S	T	U
V	W	X	Y	Z

PRINT SPC
AND PRINT TAB

The PRINT SPC and PRINT TAB commands provide additional flexibility when printing output. The abbreviation SPC stands for "space" and the abbreviation TAB stands for "tabulate." We'll take up PRINT SPC first. In this example, the program gives five spaces, then prints the asterisk.

```
010 PRINT SPC(5);"♦"
020 END

♦RUN

        ♦
```

In the next program the computer gives five blanks, prints an asterisk, gives ten additional blanks, prints a plus, finally gives five more blanks and prints an equals sign.

```
010 PRINT SPC(5);"♦";SPC(10);"+";SPC(5);"="
020 END

♦RUN

     ♦          +     =
```

The argument for the SPC function may be a number, a name, or an expression. In the following example, J tells how many blanks to place ahead of J's value.

```
010 FOR J=1 TO 10
020 PRINT SPC(J);J
030 NEXT J
040 END

◆RUN
```

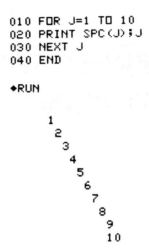

The next example shows three values being printed:

```
010 LET X=3.5
020 LET Y=4.5
030 LET Z=X+Y
040 PRINT SPC(3);X;SPC(10);Y;SPC(5);Z
050 END

◆RUN
```

```
          3.5                     4.5              8
```

The example program that follows plots the sine curve. The argument of the function SPC is computed from:

$$SIN(X) * 30 + 31$$

```
010 LET X=0
020 FOR I = 1 TO 41
030 PRINT SPC(SIN(X)◆30+31);"◆"
040 LET X=X+3.14159265/20
050 NEXT I
060 END
```

◆RUN

The TAB function causes the computer system to tabulate just like the TAB key on a typewriter. In the program that follows, the system prints the value of A then tabulates to position 30 and prints the value of B; it then tabulates to position 50 and prints the value of C. The value of A is therefore printed where it would normally print, but the values of B and C are printed where the user specifies. Note that the A value has no TAB associated with it.

```
010 LET A=4.5
020 LET B=5.6
030 LET C=2.4
040 PRINT A,TAB(30);B;TAB(50);C
050 END
```

◆RUN

```
        4.5                     5.6                     2.4
```

When tabulating, the argument given for the TAB function may be a number, a name, or an expression. Tabulating may proceed only from left to right. Backwards tabbing is illegal and an attempt to tabulate backwards will give incorrect output. The program that follows shows the values 1, 2, 3, 4, and 5 being printed.

```
010 FOR K=1 TO 5
020 PRINT TAB(K);K
030 NEXT K
040 END

◆RUN
```

```
  1
   2
    3
     4
      5
```

Another example is

```
010 FOR K=1 TO 5
020 PRINT TAB(K);"◆"
030 NEXT K
040 END

◆RUN
```

```
  ◆
   ◆
    ◆
     ◆
      ◆
```

and another would be

```
010 PRINT TAB(5);"◆";TAB(15);"+";TAB(22);"="
020 END

◆RUN
```

```
    ◆         +       =
```

In order to do precise tabulating, one should be aware of the fact that print positions begin at 1 and increase toward the maximum permitted by the terminal. In the program that follows, the sine curve is plotted. Observe the .5 added to P in the calculation at line 040. This addition rounds the computed print position, P.

```
010 LET X=0
020 FOR N=1 TO 21
030 LET K=SIN(X)
040 LET P=K*16+18+.5
050 PRINT TAB(P);"*"
060 LET X=X+3.14159265/10
070 NEXT N
080 END

*RUN
```

The next program superimposes the sine and cosine curves. At line 070, the two computed print positions are tested to make sure that tabulating proceeds from left to right. Two PRINT TAB commands are given, one when P is less than P1, and the other when P1 is less than or equal to P.

```
010 LET X=0
020 FOR N=1 TO 21
030 LET K=SIN(X)
040 LET K1=COS(X)
050 LET P=K*16+18+.5
060 LET P1=K1*16+18+.5
070 IF P1<P THEN 100
080 PRINT TAB(P);"*";TAB(P1);"+"
090 GO TO 110
100 PRINT TAB(P1);"+";TAB(P);"*"
110 LET X=X+3.14159265/10
120 NEXT N
130 END

*RUN
```

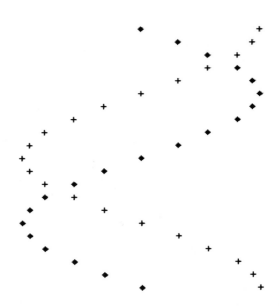

The next program plots values found in a DATA statement. It is known that those values lie between 1 and 50. Therefore, the values themselves can be used directly as the arguments in the PRINT TAB statement.

```
010 DATA 3,5,7,8,7,6,9,19,23,30
020 DATA 31,33,35,36,35,33,37,39,43
030 DATA 1000
040 READ X
050 IF X=1000 THEN 80
060 PRINT TAB(X+.5);"*"
070 GO TO 40
080 END
```

◆RUN

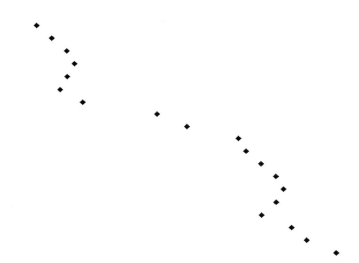

The next example shows how a wider range of values in a DATA statement can be plotted. The print position for each value is computed using the relationship:

$$P = \left[\frac{X - 40}{R} \times 60 \right] + .5$$

The largest value expected in the DATA statement is 90. R, the "range" of values, is computed from 90 - 40. The value, 60, in the equation tells how many print positions of the report line we wish to use when plotting the data. In words, the above formula can be expressed as:

$$\text{Print-position} = \left[\frac{\text{data-value} - \text{smallest-value}}{\text{Range}} \times \text{line-length} \right] + .5$$

```
010 PRINT "40      45      50      55      60      65      70      75";
020 PRINT "      80      85      90"
030 DATA 45,46,50,55,59,63,60,55,63,75
040 DATA 77,79,83,80,79,85,87,88,89
050 DATA 1000
060 LET R=90-40
070 READ X
080 IF X=1000 THEN 120
090 LET P=((X-40)/R)◆60+.5
100 PRINT TAB(P);"◆"
110 GO TO 70
120 END
```

◆RUN

EXERCISES

1. What does the PRINT SPC command accomplish?
2. Study this command:

    PRINT SPC (6); "*"; SPC (10); "="

    In what print position will the equals sign print?
3. What are the three forms of arguments that the PRINT SPC command may employ?
4. Show the output given by this program:

    ```
    10 FOR N = 1 TO 3
    20 PRINT SPC(3);N
    30 NEXT N
    40 END
    ```

5. What does the PRINT TAB command accomplish?
6. What are the three forms of arguments that the PRINT TAB command may employ?
7. Show the output given by this program:

```
10  FOR N = 1 TO 3
20  PRINT TAB(5); N
30  NEXT N
40  END
```

8. Study the program that follows:

```
10  LET B = 7.6
20  PRINT TAB(10); B; TAB(20); B ↑ 2
30  END
```

In what print positions will B and B ↑ 2 begin?

9. Write a program that plots the data given in this data statement:

    DATA 18,10,3,7,16,31,46,43,49,47

10. Write a program that plots the data given in this data statement:

    DATA 36,51,73,105,90,85,100,120,135,124

11. Write a program that prints this design:

```
         *
       *   *
     *   *   *
   *   * *   *
     *   *   *
       *   *
         *
```

12. Write a program that prints this design:

```
    * * * * * *
    * * * * * *
    * * *
    * * * * * *
        * * *
    * * * * * *
    * * * * * *
```

PRINT USING

The PRINT USING command enables one to position answers precisely on output paper. Example:

```
010 LET X=3.456
020 PRINT USING 30,X
030 :    #.##
040 END

◆RUN

     3.46
```

The computer system prints the value of X as formatted by lines 020 and 030. The pound sign (#) indicates places for digits. The decimal point given shows where the number's actual decimal point is to be positioned. Observe that the output value is rounded.

The next example shows some extra blanks placed between line 030 and the colon. The positions immediately following the colon represent print positions 1, 2, 3, etc.

```
010 LET X=3.456
020 PRINT USING 30,X
030       : #.##
040 END

◆RUN

    3.46
```

Zeroes are used to fill out decimal places if necessary. Leading unused pound signs are given as blanks. Example:

```
010 LET X=3.456
020 PRINT USING 30,X
030:      #####.#####
040 END

◆RUN


          3.45600
```

Note that the colon may be given immediately following a line number.   Decimal values can be rounded to integers if desired. Example:

```
010 LET X=3.456
020 PRINT USING 30,X
030 :     ####
040 END

◆RUN


          3
```

If a value can't be fit into the space allowed, the computer system gives asterisks instead of digits. In the following example, there is no room for the integer portion of the answer.

```
010 LET X=3.456
020 PRINT USING 30,X
030 :      .##
040 END

◆RUN


          ◆◆◆
```

Extra output images that are not needed are ignored by the system. Example:

```
010 LET X=3.456
020 PRINT USING 30,X
030 :    #.##       #.##
040 END

◆RUN


      3.46
```

But if a required output image is not given, the system gives a string of asterisks:

```
010 LET X=3.456
015 Y=45.66
020 PRINT USING 30,X,Y
030 :    #.##
040 END

◆RUN


      3.46   ◆◆◆◆
```

The computer system prints any characters given which are not pound signs (#), up arrows (↑), or apostrophes ('). Example:

```
010 LET X=3.456
015 LET Y=45.66
020 PRINT USING 30,X,Y
030 : THE VALUE OF X IS #.##, AND THE VALUE OF Y IS $##.##
040 END

◆RUN


 THE VALUE OF X IS 3.46, AND THE VALUE OF Y IS $45.66
```

Here is another example of characters being printed literally:

```
010 PRINT USING 20
020 : ABCDEFGHIJKLMNOPQRSTUVWXYZ 0123456789 !"$%&() ◆:=-
030 END

◆RUN


 ABCDEFGHIJKLMNOPQRSTUVWXYZ 0123456789 !"$%&() ◆:=-
```

The next example shows that the output image may appear
anywhere in a program:

```
010 :    ##.##
020 LET X=35.67
030 PRINT USING 10,X
040 END

◆RUN


    35.67
```

Observe that a place must be allowed for a minus sign if a value
is negative:

```
010 :    ###.##
020 LET X=-35.67
030 PRINT USING 10,X
040 END

◆RUN


    -35.67
```

A series of four up arrows indicates that answers are to be
given in exponential notation:

```
010 LET X=34.56
020 LET Y=24.56
030 LET Z=X^Y
040 PRINT USING 50,X,Y,Z
050 :   ##.##    ##.##    #.######^^^^
060 END

◆RUN


    34.56    24.56    6.128733E 37
```

Here is another example:

```
010 LET X=34.56
020 LET Y=24.56
030 LET Z=X^Y
040 PRINT USING 50,X,Y,Z
050 :   #.###^^^^    #.###^^^^    ##.#####^^^^
060 END
```

◆RUN

       3.456E 01   2.456E 01   61.28733E 36

At least one digit must be requested ahead of the decimal point.
Note this next example which violates the rule about requesting at
least one digit ahead of the decimal point.

```
010 LET X=34.56
020 LET Y=24.56
030 LET Z=X^Y
040 PRINT USING 50,X,Y,Z
050 :     .####^^^^     .####^^^^     .#######^^^^
060 END
```

◆RUN

     ◆◆◆◆◆◆◆◆◆   ◆◆◆◆◆◆◆◆◆   ◆◆◆◆◆◆◆◆◆◆◆◆

If a value is negative, two pound signs must be given ahead of the
decimal point as shown below. Note that the value of X does not
print because a pound sign was not given to cover the negative sign.

```
010 LET X=-34.56
020 LET Y=24.56
030 LET Z=X◆Y
040 PRINT USING 50,X,Y,Z
050 :   #.###^^^^    #.###^^^^    ##.######^^^^
060 END
```

◆RUN

     ◆◆◆◆◆◆◆◆◆   2.456E 01   -8.487936E 02

Powers are sometimes negative:

```
010 LET X=34.56
020 LET Y=.00000002456
030 LET Z=X^Y
040 PRINT USING 50,X,Y,Z
050 :   ##.##^^^^    ##.##^^^^    ##.#####^^^^
060 END
```

◆RUN

     34.56E 00   24.56E-09   10.00000E-01

If four up arrows are not given, incorrect output is received:

```
010 LET X=34.56
020 LET Y=.00000002456
030 LET Z=X^Y
040 PRINT USING 50,X,Y,Z
050 :   ##.##^^^      ##.##^^      ##.####^
060 END

◆RUN


    34.56^^^        .00^^       1.0000^
```

Output provided by alphanumeric variables is preceded by an apostrophe and a series of L's. In the example that follows, not enough L's have been given. Only the leftmost six characters of the message held by A$ are printed.

```
010 LET A$="TYPE IN THE DATA"
020 PRINT USING 30,A$
030 :       'LLLLL
040 END

◆RUN


    TYPE I
```

The message makes more sense when the string of L's is increased:

```
010 LET A$="TYPE IN THE DATA"
020 PRINT USING 30,A$
030 :'LLLLLLLLLLLLLLLLLLLL
040 END

◆RUN

TYPE IN THE DATA
```

R's may be used as well as L's. (R means right adjustment, L means left adjustment.)

```
010 LET A$="TYPE IN THE DATA"
020 PRINT USING 30,A$
030 : ´RRRRRRRRRRRRRRRRRRRRRRRRRRRRRRRRRRRRRRRRRRRR
040 END
```

◆RUN

                    TYPE IN THE DATA

Observe that the values are right adjusted in the space allowed by
the string of R's. C's cause centering:

```
010 LET A$="TYPE IN THE DATA"
020 PRINT USING 30,A$
030:´CCCCCCCCCCCCCCCCCCCCCCCCCCCCCCCCCCCCCCCCCCCCCCCCCCCCCCCCCCCCCCC
040 END
```

◆RUN

            TYPE IN THE DATA

EXERCISES

1. What does the PRINT USING command accomplish?
2. Study this example:

          20 PRINT USING 40,A
          40:     #.##

    Where will the value that A holds be printed?
3. Tell what's wrong, if anything, in this next example:

          50 PRINT USING 80,A,B
          80:     ##.##

4. Study this example:

          100 PRINT USING 110, E
          110   :   ##.##

    Where will E's value print?

5. Study this example:

> 110   PRINT USING 120,G
> 120: $##.##

What will print if G's value is 25.85?

6. Study this example:

> 200   PRINT USING 300
> 300:   COST REPORT

What will the computer print? Where?

7. What do up arrows (↑) do in a PRINT USING line? Example:

> 15   PRINT USING 20,F
> 20:   #.##↑↑↑↑

8. Study this example:

> 50   PRINT USING 60,D
> 60:   ###.##

What will the computer system print if D's value is −38.47?
Where?

9. When would you use 'LLLLLLL in a PRINT USING line?

10. What does 'RRRRR accomplish when you use it in a PRINT
USING line?

11. What does 'CCCCCCCCCC accomplish when you use it in a
PRINT USING line?

12. Study this example:

> 200   PRINT USING 300,H
> 300:   ##.#

What will the computer system print if H's value is 305.6?

FILES

A file is an organized collection of data concerning some given subject. Files provide BASIC programs with sources of values that can be used as input data. Up to this point, we have used only the DATA/READ and INPUT statements to provide input. In this chapter, you'll see how to create data files and how to read and write using files. First, to create a file, you can type a series of data lines and save them under some arbitrary name. Example:

```
NEW
NEW FILE NAME--DATAFILE
READY
10 4,    5,    8,
20 9,    4,    2,
30 9,    3,    6,
SAVE
DATA SAVED-DATAFILE
```

The file named DATAFILE has been created. It consists of three lines. Each line begins with a line number that is followed by three data values. Each data value is followed by a comma. The name of a file may consist of from 1 to 8 alphabetic characters.

The next program shows how the data values in DATAFILE can be read. A listing of the input file is also shown so that you can compare the file's contents with the printout.

```
10 FILES DATAFILE
20 IF END #1 THEN 60
30 READ #1,A,B,C
40 PRINT A,B,C
50 GO TO 20
60 END

◆RUN


        4              5              8
        9              4              2
        9              3              6


◆OLD DATAFILE
◆LIST

10 4,     5,     8,
20 9,     4,     2,
30 9,     3,     6,
```

The FILES statement gives the names of all the files used in the program. This program uses only one file, DATAFILE. The program gives the command:

30 READ #1, A, B, C

File #1 is DATAFILE. Before the file is read, the command:

20 IF END #1 THEN 60

tests the file to determine whether the file contains values to be read. If the answer is "yes," the program goes to the READ statement. If "no," the program goes to line 60. That is, the program jumps to line 60 if there is an end-of-file in file #1.

Study the program and the file, DATAFILE. The program reads the file one line at a time and prints it. When the program finds an end-of-file condition in DATAFILE, it jumps to line 60 and stops. Line numbers in a file are ignored when a file is read.

The next program uses two files, DATAFILE and OUTFILE. In the program, DATAFILE is file #1, and OUTFILE is file #2. The sequence of file names in the FILES statement determines which is file #1 and which is file #2. The program reads data from DATAFILE and writes lines into OUTFILE. Observe that the SCRATCH command must be given to enable the writing into a file. A file must be prepared for writing so that the computer will not accidently write into it. This preparation is accomplished with the SCRATCH command. (Normally, all files are initially in READ mode; the SCRATCH COMMAND changes a file from READ to WRITE mode.)

```
010 FILES DATAFILE;OUTFILE
020 SCRATCH #2
030 IF END #1 THEN 70
040 READ #1,A,B,C
050 WRITE #2,A,B,C
060 GO TO 30
070 PRINT "END OF RUN"
080 END

◆RUN


END OF RUN

◆OLD
OLD FILE? OUTFILE
◆LIST

000010          4,          5,          8,
000020          9,          4,          2,
000030          9,          3,          6,


◆OLD DATAFILE
◆LIST

10 4,    5,    8,
20 9,    4,    2,
30 9,    3,    6,
```

Observe that the program prints only one line:

    END OF RUN

The program writes lines into an output file. To determine what has been written into the file, you must list the file. Observe that when the system creates a file it automatically supplies line numbers. Note also, that *input* files must have a comma entered after every data item. Files that the computer system writes also include commas after every data item.

Values written into a file can be written with less space between numbers by placing semicolons rather than commas in the WRITE statement. An example follows on the next page.

```
010 FILES DATAFILE;OUTFILE
020 SCRATCH #2
030 IF END #1 THEN 70
040 READ #1,A,B,C
050 WRITE #2,A;B;C
060 GO TO 30
070 PRINT "END OF RUN"
080 END

◆RUN


END OF RUN

◆OLD OUTFILE
◆LIST

000010        4,      5,      8,
000020        9,      4,      2,
000030        9,      3,      6,


◆OLD DATAFILE
◆LIST

10 4,    5,    8,
20 9,    4,    2,
30 9,    3,    6,
```

Files can be created without line numbers if desired.   The
PRINT # command is given rather than the WRITE # command.
Example:

```
010 FILES DATAFILE;OUTFILE
020 SCRATCH #2
030 IF END #1 THEN 70
040 READ #1,A,B,C
050 PRINT #2,A;B;C
060 GO TO 30
070 PRINT "END OF RUN"
080 END

◆RUN


END OF RUN

◆OLD OUTFILE
◆LIST

    4       5       8
    9       4       2
    9       3       6
```

```
◆OLD DATAFILE
◆LIST

10 4,    5,    8,
20 9,    4,    2,
30 9,    3,    6,
```

Note that the output file has no commas following each data value.

The next example shows some values being read from DATAFILE, a calculation being made, and OUTFILE being written.

```
010 FILES DATAFILE;OUTFILE
020 SCRATCH #2
030 IF END #1 THEN 80
040 READ #1,A,B,C
050 LET D=A*B*C
060 PRINT #2,A;B;C;D
070 GO TO 30
080 PRINT "END OF RUN"
090 END

◆RUN

END OF RUN

◆OLD OUTFILE
◆LIST

    4    5    8   160
    9    4    2    72
    9    3    6   162


◆OLD DATAFILE
◆LIST

10 4,    5,    8,
20 9,    4,    2,
30 9,    3,    6,
```

The following example shows that, after a file has been written, it can be read. To read a file that has been written, the RESTORE command must be given. This output file is changed from WRITE mode to READ mode. This example shows how one line could be read from a file that was created earlier in the same program.

```
010 FILES DATAFILE;OUTFILE
020 SCRATCH #2
030 IF END #1 THEN 80
040 READ #1,A,B,C
050 LET D=A*B*C
060 WRITE #2,A;B;C;D
070 GO TO 30
080 RESTORE #2
090 READ #2,U,V,W,X
100 PRINT U;V;W;X
110 END
```

◆RUN

        4   5   8   160

◆OLD OUTFILE
◆LIST

```
000010        4,       5,       8,     160,
000020        9,       4,       2,      72,
000030        9,       3,       6,     162,
```

◆OLD DATAFILE
◆LIST

```
10 4,      5,       8,
20 9,      4,       2,
30 9,      3,       6,
```

The next example shows the "backspacing" of data items. The program reads values 4, 5, 8, and 9, assigning them to A, B, C, and D. The program prepares itself to read the next value, 4. Backspacing twice brings the system back to 8. The value is read, assigned to X, then printed.

```
010 FILES DATAFILE
020 READ #1,A,B,C,D
030 PRINT A;B;C;D
040 BACKSPACE #1
050 BACKSPACE #1
060 READ #1,X
070 PRINT X
080 END
```

◆RUN

        4   5   8   9
                8

```
◆OLD DATAFILE
◆LIST

10 4,    5,    8,
20 9,    4,    2,
30 9,    3,    6,
```

To restore a file (using RESTORE) also means to reposition a pointer to the beginning value of the file. Observe how the first value in DATAFILE is reread.

```
010 FILES DATAFILE
020 READ #1,A,B,C,D
030 PRINT A;B;C;D
040 RESTORE #1
050 READ #1,X
060 PRINT X
070 END

◆RUN

     4    5    8    9
          4

◆OLD DATAFILE
◆LIST

10 4,    5,    8,
20 9,    4,    2,
30 9,    3,    6,
```

The next example shows the merging of two files—FILEA and FILEB—into FILEC. The two input files are these:

```
◆LIST FILEA

10 215,    34,    59,
20 220,    45,    67,
30 228,    37,    21,
40 236,    87,    26,
50 246,    33,    60,
60 257,    35,    76,

◆LIST FILEB

10 213,    80,    24,
20 214,    31,    30,
30 223,    63,    93,
40 256,    43,    75,
50 259,    25,    27,
```

The program that merges the two files is this:

```
010 FILES FILEA;FILEB;FILEC
020 SCRATCH #3
030 LET S=1
040 IF END #1 THEN 190
050 READ #1,K1,X1,Y1
060 IF S=1 THEN 80
070 GO TO 110
080 LET S=0
090 IF END #2 THEN 160
100 READ #2,K2,X2,Y2
110 IF K1<K2 THEN 140
120 WRITE #3,K2;X2;Y2
130 GO TO 90
140 WRITE #3,K1;X1;Y1
150 GO TO 40
160 LET K2=999
170 IF K1=999 THEN 220
180 GO TO 110
190 LET K1=999
200 IF K2=999 THEN 220
210 GO TO 110
220 PRINT "JOB COMPLETE"
230 END
```

```
◆RUN


JOB COMPLETE
```

A listing of files FILEA, FILEB, and FILEC follows.

```
◆OLD FILEC
◆LIST

000010     213,     80,     24,
000020     214,     31,     30,
000030     215,     34,     59,
000040     220,     45,     67,
000050     223,     63,     93,
000060     228,     37,     21,
000070     236,     87,     26,
000080     246,     33,     60,
000090     256,     43,     75,
000100     257,     35,     76,
000110     259,     25,     27,


◆OLD FILEA
◆LIST
```

```
10 215,    34,    59,
20 220,    45,    67,
30 228,    37,    21,
40 236,    87,    26,
50 246,    33,    60,
60 257,    35,    76,


◆OLD FILEB
◆LIST

10 213,    80,    24,
20 214,    31,    30,
30 223,    63,    93,
40 256,    43,    75,
50 259,    25,    27,
```

Study the program carefully to see how merging is accomplished.

EXERCISES

1. Define the term *file*.
2. What does the expression "read a file" mean?
3. What does the command

   IF END #1 THEN . . . . .

   mean? Why would you give this command ahead of a file READ command?
4. Study this portion of a BASIC program:

   ```
   10 FILES X-FILE; Y-FILE
   20 IF END #2 THEN 80
   30 READ #2,A,B,C
        .
        .
        .
        .
   ```

   What is the name of the file from which data are being read?
5. What is wrong with the file that begins below?

   ```
   10 8.6  3.5  4.2
   ```

```
20  9.7  1.2  7.5
30  8.5  9.6  9.8
40  7.6  8.1  1.3
```

6. Refer to Question 5. What might be a valid name that you would invent for the file?

7. What does the SCRATCH command accomplish?

8. What is meant by the statement that files are initially in READ mode? What is WRITE mode?

9. If a program contained the two commands:

    WRITE #3,X,Y,Z   and   PRINT #3,X,Y,Z

    how would the two commands differ?

10. How could a file be read after it has been completely written?

11. What command "backspaces" files?

12. What does the RESTORE command accomplish? (Example: RESTORE #2)

13. Write a program that reads values from a file named INPUT3 and writes those values into a file named OUTPUT4. Here is what INPUT3 looks like:

```
10   9.6,   1.8,   3.7,   9.9,
20  -7.8,  -9.2,  -8.2,  -8.3,
30   3.4,   7.7,   1.4,   1.2,
40   7.6,   1.4,   7.4,   9.5,
```

14. Study this program. List all the errors that you see:

```
10 FILES DATAF,OUTF
20 SCRATCH #1
30 IF END #1 THEN GO TO 70
40 READ #1,A;B;C
50 WRITE #2,A,B,C
60 GO TO 10
70 GO TO 30
80 PRINT "END OF RUN"
90 END
```

DEFINED FUNCTIONS

BASIC makes available several functions. You've seen most of them: SIN, COS, TAN, SQR, LOG, EXP, ABS, INT, RND. You may, however, require a function that is not built into the BASIC language. You can define your own. Example:

```
010 DATA 2,7,6,5,1,1000
020 DEF SUM(X)=X+X
030 READ X
040 IF X=1000 THEN 80
050 LET A=SUM(X)
060 PRINT A
070 GO TO 30
080 END

◆RUN


        4
       14
       12
       10
        2
```

The new function SUM has been defined. It adds a value to itself; that is, the function doubles any value given to it. When one defines a function, one gives the statement beginning with DEF. Then, the individual invents a name for this "homemade" function. The name must have three characters. Giving one or more arguments in parentheses, the user then defines what the function does with those arguments. Later in the program, the user employs the defined function with all the flexibility of a built-in function.

In this next example, the name of the defined function is SNH. The function obtains the hyperbolic sine. It does so by utilizing this relationship:

$$\sinh = \frac{e^x - e^{-x}}{2}$$

```
010 DEF SNH(X)=(EXP(X)-EXP(-X))/2
020 INPUT X
030 IF X=1000 THEN 70
040 LET A=SNH(X)
050 PRINT A
060 GO TO 20
070 END

◆RUN


?-1
    -1.175201
?1
     1.175201
?10
     11013.23
?1000
```

Observe that the program computes the hyperbolic sine of various values of X that are input into the program.

The next program uses a function having two arguments. Those arguments are A and B.

```
010 DEF XYZ(A,B)=A^2/B^3
020 INPUT A,B
030 IF A=0 THEN 70
040 LET C=XYZ(A,B)
050 PRINT C
060 GO TO 20
070 END

◆RUN
```

```
?4,5
            .128
?9,.5
            648
?2,20
          .0005
?.1,.001
        10000000
?0,0
```

Here is another example of the function XYZ in use. Note that function XYZ can be used in the same expression that uses a built-in function.

```
010 DEF XYZ(A,B)=A^2/B^3
020 INPUT A,B
030 IF A=0 THEN 70
040 LET C=SIN(A)+COS(B)+XYZ(A,B)
050 PRINT C
060 GO TO 20
070 END

◆RUN


?8,2
      8.573211
?10,4
      .3648353
?0,0
```

The next program uses two defined functions, XYZ and PDQ.

```
010 DEF XYZ(A,B)=A^2/B^3
015 DEF PDQ(F)=F^4
020 INPUT A,B,F
030 IF A=0 THEN 70
040 LET A=XYZ(A,B)/PDQ(F)
050 PRINT A
060 GO TO 20
070 END

◆RUN


?9,7,2
      .0147595
?.01,1,.001
      1.00000E 08
?0,0,0
```

The variable name(s) used in function definitions are "dummies." They are place holders for the *actual* arguments given when the homemade function is used. When using a function, the actual arguments given do not have to match the dummy names. Example:

```
010 DEF XYZ(A,B)=A^2/B^3
015 DEF PDQ(F)=F^4
020 INPUT R,S,T
030 IF R=0 THEN 70
040 LET C=XYZ(R,S)/PDQ(T)
050 PRINT C
060 GO TO 20
070 END

◆RUN


?9,7,2
     .0147595
?.01,1,.001
     1.00000E 08
?0,0,0
```

This is the same program as the one given earlier. The dummy names used in the function definitions are A, B, and F. The actual values used are R, S, and T. The actual argument, R, is substituted for the dummy, A; the actual, S, for the dummy, B; and the actual, T, for the dummy F.

When using a defined function, you may use actual arguments consisting of numbers, names, and/or expressions. The two functions above could be used this way, for example:

```
010 DEF XYZ(A,B)=A^2/B^3
020 DEF PDQ(F)=F^4
030 LET Q=6.2
040 LET C=XYZ(Q,3.5)/PDQ((Q+5.6)/3)
050 PRINT C
060 END

◆RUN


     .0037457
```

The actual argument, Q, matches the dummy, A; the actual, 3.5, matches the dummy, B; and the actual (Q + 5.6)/3 matches the dummy, F.

If a function requires more than one statement to define, the definition begins with DEF and ends with FNEND. Observe that the next program uses the defined function DDT. The definition begins at line 010 and ends at line 035. In the function definition, the name of the function must appear at least once on the lefthand side of an equals sign. That is how the function actually receives its value.

```
010 DEF DDT(A,B)
015 IF A>B THEN 30
020 DDT=A+B
025 GO TO 35
030 DDT=A-B
035 FNEND
040 DATA 4,9,3,9,6,5,5,2,0,0
045 READ X,Y
050 IF X=0 THEN 70
055 C=DDT(X,Y)
060 PRINT X;Y;C
065 GO TO 45
070 END

◆RUN
```

```
4    9    13
3    9    12
6    5     1
5    2     3
```

EXERCISES

1. Give the names of nine functions that are built into the BASIC language. Two of them, for example, are SIN and SQR.

2. What is a homemade function?

3. What are the three forms of arguments that you may employ when you call for the use of a defined (homemade) function?

4. What three characters must you use just ahead of a homemade function definition—ahead of the function's name?

5. May a defined function consist of more than one coding line?

6. Show how you would define a function that makes this next calculation:

$$\frac{W + 9.6}{W^2}$$

Name the function WCC.

7. Show how you would define a function that makes this calculation:

$$\frac{b + c}{b + 5.8}$$

Name the function BCC.

8. What is meant by the statement that in the definition of a function, the variable names given are "dummies"?

9. Tell what is wrong with this function definition entry in a BASIC program:

   DEF RTL(X,Y) = (X + 1.3)/2.7

10. Tell what is wrong with this function entry in a BASIC program:

    DEF JOE(B) = (A + B) / (A - 5.8)

11. Study this program:

    ```
    10 DEF CAL (A,B) = (A * B) / (A + B)
    20 INPUT P,Q
    30 IF P = 100 THEN 70
    40 R = CAL (P,Q) + 2
    50 PRINT P,Q,R
    60 GO TO 20
    70 END
    ```

    What will the program print as the value for R when P's value is 2 and Q's value is 4?

12. Study this program:

    ```
    010 DEF RED (P,Q)
    020 IF P > Q THEN 50
    030 RED = P * Q
    ```

```
040 GO TO 60
050 RED = P / Q
060 FNEND
070 INPUT W,X
080 Z = RED (W,X)
090 PRINT Z
100 END
```

What will the program print as the value for 2 when W's value is 24 and X's value is 2?

THE CHANGE STATEMENT

The CHANGE statement is used to convert an alphanumeric string of characters to individual numeric codes or vice versa. A string is a series of characters—letters of the alphabet, digits, and special characters. As an example, consider the program that follows:

```
10 DIM X(16)
20 LET A$="TYPE IN THE DATA"
30 CHANGE A$ TO X
40 FOR J= 0 TO 16
50 PRINT X(J)
60 NEXT J
70 END

◆RUN

        16
        84
        89
        80
        69
        32
        73
        78
        32
        84
        72
        69
        32
        68
        65
        84
        65
```

Each of the sixteen characters of the message

TYPE IN THE DATA

has been converted to a numeric code and those codes have been
stored into the array X. The numeric code for T is 84; for Y, 89;
for P, 80; etc. Those codes are stored in X_1 through X_{16}. In X_0
the count of the characters (16) of the message is stored.

The reverse process is possible. Example:

```
010 DIM X(20)
020 LET X(0) = 5
030 LET X(1) = 66
040 LET X(2) = 65
050 LET X(3) = 83
060 LET X(4) = 73
070 LET X(5) = 67
080 CHANGE X TO W$
090 PRINT W$
100 END

◆RUN


BASIC
```

At line 020 the count of characters is stored at X_0. That count is
5. Then at X_1 through X_5 the numeric codes for the characters
B, A, S, I, C, are stored. These codes are 66, 65, 83, 73, and 67.
The CHANGE statement at line 080 converts the five codes stored
in X_1 through X_5 to alphabetic characters and joins them together
to form W$. It can be seen that the word BASIC has been assigned
to W$.

In this next program, the codes 32 through 94 are stored in
the array X_1 through X_{63}. Then the array X is converted to a
character variable A$ and printed. Observe that the number 63 is
stored into X_0. This gives the count of characters that were stored
in A$.

```
010 DIM X(63)
020 FOR I=1 TO 63
030 LET X(I) = I+31
040 NEXT I
050 LET X(0) = 63
060 CHANGE X TO A$
070 PRINT A$
080 END
```

◆RUN

! "#$%&'()♦+,-./0123456789:;<=>?@ABCDEFGHIJKLMNOPQRSTUVWXYZ[\]^

In the example that follows, each of the characters shown in the output is printed along with its respective numeric code. The numeric code for "blank" is 32; for !, 33; for ", 34; for #, 35; etc. The program gives a table of various data processing characters along with their numeric codes.

```
010 DIM X(63)
015 FOR I=1 TO 63
020 LET X(I)=I+31
025 NEXT I
030 LET X(0) = 1
035 FOR J=1 TO 63
040 LET X(1)=X(J)
045 CHANGE X TO A$
050 PRINT USING 55,A$,X(J),
055 :       'L  ##       'L  ##       'L  ##       'L  ##
060 NEXT J
065 END
```

◆RUN

	32	!	33	"	34	#	35
$	36	%	37	&	38	'	39
(	40	)	41	♦	42	+	43
,	44	-	45	.	46	/	47
0	48	1	49	2	50	3	51
4	52	5	53	6	54	7	55
8	56	9	57	:	58	;	59
<	60	=	61	>	62	?	63
@	64	A	65	B	66	C	67
D	68	E	69	F	70	G	71
H	72	I	73	J	74	K	75
L	76	M	77	N	78	O	79
P	80	Q	81	R	82	S	83
T	84	U	85	V	86	W	87
X	88	Y	89	Z	90	[	91
\	92	]	93	^	94		

The CHANGE statement at line 045 converts a single numeric code to its alphanumeric equivalent. The character, as well as its numeric equivalent is printed. Since the CHANGE statement is in a loop that is executed 63 times, 63 characters are printed, along with their numeric codes.

The object of the next program is to ring the terminal's bell ten times. The program converts the code 7 to a character in A$. This code rings a bell on a terminal. The program prints A$. Each time, the terminal's bell rings or gives a beep depending upon the terminal being used.

```
010 DIM X(20)
020 LET X(0) = 1
030 LET X(1) = 7
040 FOR J = 1 TO 10
050 CHANGE X TO A$
060 PRINT A$;
070 NEXT J
080 END


◆RUN
```

Another way to ring the bell ten times is shown below. Code 7 is assigned to X_1 through X_{10}. The number 10 is assigned to X_0. The array X is changed to A\$ and A\$ is printed once. The bell rings ten times.

```
010 DIM X(2)
020 FOR Q=1 TO 10
030 LET X(0)=1
040 LET X(1)=7
050 CHANGE X TO A$
060 PRINT A$
070 NEXT Q
080 END


◆RUN
```

The following program requests a message to be input from the terminal. (See line 030.) Then it finds a three-character key word in that message as input at line 050.

```
010 DIM X(100)
020 DIM Y(3)
030 INPUT A$
040 IF A$="DONE" THEN 230
050 CHANGE A$ TO X
060 INPUT B$
070 CHANGE B$ TO Y
080 FOR J=1 TO X(0)-2
090 IF Y(1)=X(J) THEN 110
100 GO TO 180
110 IF Y(2)=X(J+1) THEN 130
120 GO TO 180
130 IF Y(3)=X(J+2) THEN 150
140 GO TO 180
150 PRINT "FOUND ´";B$;"´ AT LOCATIONS";J;J+1;J+2;"OF:"
160 PRINT "´";A$;"´"
170 GO TO 210
180 NEXT J
190 PRINT "THE VALUE ´";B$;"´ IS NOT IN THE VALUE:"
```

```
200 PRINT "´";A$;"´"
210 PRINT
220 GO TO 30
230 END

◆RUN

?THIS IS THE MESSAGE IN WHICH WE WILL TRY TO FIND A KEY WORD
?KEY
FOUND ´KEY´ AT LOCATIONS   52    53    54 OF:
´THIS IS THE MESSAGE IN WHICH WE WILL TRY TO FIND A KEY WORD´

?THIS IS ANOTHER ONE
?ONE
FOUND ´ONE´ AT LOCATIONS   17    18    19 OF:
´THIS IS ANOTHER ONE´

?AND STILL ANOTHER
?AND
FOUND ´AND´ AT LOCATIONS    1     2     3 OF:
´AND STILL ANOTHER´

?ONE MORE
?E M
FOUND ´E M´ AT LOCATIONS    3     4     5 OF:
´ONE MORE´

?DONE
```

A different version of the program is shown below. The program finds a word or series of words in the given message.

```
010 DIM X(100)
020 DIM Y(100)
030 INPUT A$
040 IF A$="DONE" THEN 220
050 CHANGE A$ TO X
060 INPUT B$
070 CHANGE B$ TO Y
080 FOR J=1 TO X(0)
090 LET N=J
100 FOR K=1 TO Y(0)
110 IF Y(K)<>X(N) GO TO 170
120 LET N=N+1
130 NEXT K
140 PRINT "FOUND ´";B$;"´ BEGINNING AT LOCATION";J;"IN:"
150 PRINT "´";A$;"´"
160 GO TO 200
170 NEXT J
180 PRINT "THE VALUE ´";B$;"´ IS NOT IN THE VALUE:"
190 PRINT "´";A$;"´"
200 PRINT
210 GO TO 30
220 END

◆RUN

?THIS IS THE MESSAGE IN WHICH WE WILL TRY TO FIND A KEY WORD
?KEY
FOUND ´KEY´ BEGINNING AT LOCATION   52 IN:
´THIS IS THE MESSAGE IN WHICH WE WILL TRY TO FIND A KEY WORD´
```

```
?THIS IS ANSOTHER MESSAGE WITH A MISSPELLED WORD
?ANSOTHER
FOUND 'ANSOTHER' BEGINNING AT LOCATION     9 IN:
'THIS IS ANSOTHER MESSAGE WITH A MISSPELLED WORD'

?ANOTHER
?THE
FOUND 'THE' BEGINNING AT LOCATION     4 IN:
'ANOTHER'

?WE WILL NOT FIND THE WORD
?KNOT
THE VALUE 'KNOT' IS NOT IN THE VALUE:
'WE WILL NOT FIND THE WORD'

?WE WILL FIND THE ENTIRE MESSAGE
?WE WILL FIND THE ENTIRE MESSAGE
FOUND 'WE WILL FIND THE ENTIRE MESSAGE' BEGINNING AT LOCATION     1 IN:
'WE WILL FIND THE ENTIRE MESSAGE'

?DONE
```

If the word or series of words being searched for is not in the message, the program advises the user of this fact. The series of words to be found can equal the length of the original message.

EXERCISES

1. What is BASIC's definition for "string"?

2. What two possible actions can CHANGE perform in connection with a string of alphanumeric characters?

3. Why is a DIM statement needed when your program uses the CHANGE statement?
    What information does location zero in an array hold when the CHANGE command is being used?

4. Give the two-digit numeric codes that apply to the word TYPE.

5. Explain what this BASIC statement accomplishes:

    CHANGE D$ TO H

6. Explain what this BASIC statement accomplishes:

    CHANGE T TO A$

7. In Question 5, must H be an array?

8. In Question 6, must T be an array?

9. Study this program:

```
10 DIM A(100)
20 LET A(0) = 4
30 LET A(1) = 84
40 LET A(2) = 69
50 LET A(3) = 83
60 LET A(4) = 84
70 CHANGE A TO C$
80 PRINT C$
90 END
```

What will the program print?

10. Write a program that prints 26 lines. Each line is to contain one of the letters of the alphabet and its associated two-digit numeric code. Use a FOR/NEXT loop.

SOLUTIONS
FOR
EXERCISES

CHAPTER 1

1. The program computes 25 times 86 and prints the result (2150).
2. RUN is a system command. (We can tell this because it does not have a line number to the left of the word.)
3. The five symbols that BASIC uses to cause calculations are + (add), - (subtract), * (multiply), / (divide), and ↑ (raise to a power).
4. Parentheses are used to cause calculations to be performed in a sequence other than the computer's built-in hierarchy of operations.
5. Extra parentheses that are not really needed in an expression will not hurt the program. When in doubt, give extra parentheses.
6. False.
7. False.
8. Yes.
9. The smallest line number is 1, the largest is 99999. On some BASIC systems the largest line number permitted is 9999.
10. A statement is an instruction in a program. It begins with a key word such as LET, PRINT, IF, READ, GO TO. A system command is an order directly to the computer, often to do

something with a program.   Some system commands are
RUN, LIST, SAVE, PURGE.

11. The program is:

```
10 PRINT 47 * 85 - 74.8
20 END
```

or

```
10 LET A = 47 * 85 - 74.8
20 PRINT A
30 END
```

12. The program is:

```
10 PRINT 347 * 92.6 * 75
20 END
```

or

```
10 LET A = 347 * 92.6 * 75
20 PRINT A
30 END
```

13. The program is:

```
10 PRINT (84.5 / 7.3) * (7.43 / 1.2)
20 END
```

Or the calculation can be assigned to a variable name, then
printed.

14. The program is:

```
10 PRINT ((7.5 + 9.7) / 8) / (2.5 / (1.7 - 5.8)) * (9.6/(1.5 - 2.8))
20 END
```

Or the calculation can be assigned to a variable name, then
printed.

15. The program is:

```
10 PRINT (2.5 / 8.3) / 9.6
```

```
20  PRINT 2.5 / (8.3 / 9.6)
30  END
```

The results are different because of the sequence that the calculations are made in. The result of 2.5 divided by 8.3, the result divided by 9.6 is different from 2.5 divided by the *quantity* 8.3 divided by 9.6.

16. The program is:

```
10  PRINT (-2) ↑ 4
20  PRINT -2 ↑ 4
30  END
```

The results are different because -2 is raised to the fourth power in the first example, while 2 is raised to the fourth power in the second example and the result subtracted from zero.

CHAPTER 2

1. The computer sorts them in increasing sequence by line numbers.
2. The character that you use is ←. In some BASIC systems, the character is @ or \.
3. Yes, use one for every incorrect character.
4. The LIST command gives a listing of a program as it exists up to date with all corrections made.
5. The RUN command causes the program that has been entered to be run (executed).
6. A BASIC statement can be corrected by retyping it in correct form.
7. A BASIC line can be deleted by typing the line number only and then returning the carriage.
8. Either command may be given first. There is no difference as far as the final results are concerned.
9. The SAVE command causes a program that has been entered to be saved. The programmer names the program at the time that he or she saves it.
10. A line number is never given ahead (to the left of) a system command.

11. The system command BYE disconnects you from the computer. A "log off" message is given by the computer just before the disconnect occurs.

12. The word RESUBMIT is not a system command. It is not even a BASIC statement key word.

13. A system command performs some action in connection with the program that has been entered (examples: RUN, SAVE, LIST), or it performs some action in connection with the timesharing session (example: BYE).

14. The computer scans your program to determine whether it detects a typographical error (for example: PRINX) and types a listing of all such errors found.

15. A statement is inserted when the user selects a line number for the statement between two existing line numbers. The new statement is inserted between the existing statements.

16. Type line number 20, then return the carriage.

17. Type a line having a line number between 30 and 40. Example:

    35 PRINT A * B + C

18. Retype the statement at line 40 this way:

    40 PRINT P + Q * R

CHAPTER 3

1. A name would be given to a numeric value if the value were needed more than once in the program.

2. The special BASIC word is LET.

3. The statement LET A = 2.4 gives the name A to the value 2.4. Another way to say this is to state that the value 2.4 is assigned to A.

4. The statement LET B = 9.2/3.3 + A causes the value A to be added to 9.2 divided by 3.3. The result is assigned to B.

5. The statement LET A = A + 1 causes the value 1 to be added to A. The result is assigned back to A. That is, the value of A is increased by 1.

6. A variable name is a BASIC symbol to which a value can be assigned. Some examples of variable names are B, X, R5, T7.

7. In BASIC a variable name may consist of a single letter of the alphabet or a single letter followed by a single digit.

8. The program is:

   ```
   10 PRINT 5.6 * 9.4
   20 END
   ```

9. The problems are:

3X	A variable name may not begin with a digit.
P–	The symbol – is not permissible in a variable name.
X33	A variable name may consist of only two characters.
PD	The second character in a variable name may not be a letter of the alphabet.

10. The program will print 2 and 16.

11. A program might be:

    ```
    10 LET A = 3.5
    20 LET B = 9.3
    30 LET C = 4.7
    40 PRINT A + B
    50 PRINT A + C
    60 PRINT B + C + 8.7
    70 END
    ```

12. A program might be:

    ```
    10 PRINT 3.8 + 4.9 - 7.6
    20 PRINT 1.4 - 6.6 + 5.8
    30 PRINT 3.7 * 4.5 * 7.6
    40 END
    ```

CHAPTER 4

1. The READ statement causes values to be obtained from the DATA statement. Values may be obtained one at a time or in sets containing two or more values.

2. The DATA statement provides the values that are obtained by one or more READ statements in the program.

3. In a BASIC program the DATA statement may be given any-where as long as it's ahead of the END statement.

4. One may give as many DATA statements in a program as are needed to hold all the values that will be read by one or more READ statements.

5. It is a good idea to place all DATA statements either at the beginning of a BASIC program or at the end just ahead of the END statement.

6. The READ statement may obtain values from the DATA statement either one at a time or in sets of two or more. Such READ statements as READ R; READ W,X; and READ T,S,M,K are acceptable.

7. The program will give the OUT OF DATA message when all values in the DATA statement have been processed and the program attempts to read one or more additional values.

8. The program will print four output lines. Three of the lines will give values, the last line will read OUT OF DATA.

9. The program will print three output lines. Two of the lines will give values. The last line will read: OUT OF DATA. Two of the values in the DATA statement will never be used (6 and 3).

10. The new program could look like this:

```
10 DATA 8,7,4,9,2,8,6,3
20 READ X,Y,Z
30 PRINT X * Y * Z
40 GO TO 20
45 DATA 5
50 END
```

The program will now give four output lines. Three of the lines will give values. The last line will read: OUT OF DATA.

CHAPTER 5

1. Three ways that a PRINT statement might be used are these:

A. Direct the computer to print a value that has been as-signed to a variable name. Example: PRINT W.

B. Direct the computer to perform a calculation and print the result. Example: PRINT (3.5 * 9.2) + H.

C. Direct the computer to print a message. Example: PRINT "CHECK TEST DATA"

2. The computer will print (36 + 8)/11 or 4.

3. The computer will print the words "THIS IS A SAMPLE MESSAGE."

4. The computer will print the *last* values assigned to X, Y, and Z; that is, 5, 9, and 30.

5. The computer will print the letter X, the letter Y and the letter Z. There will be approximately 14 unused print positions between X and Y and between Y and Z.

6. The computer will need one print line to print the values of R, T, U, W, and Z.

7. The PRINT statement causes a single blank line to be given.

8. The computer will print the message: THE VALUE OF G IS and will also print the actual value of G. The printout will look like this:

THE VALUE OF G IS 7.7

9. The computer will print the values of R, F, H, N, and T; however, the PRINT statement at line 50 causes the values to be printed closer together.

10. Yes, the statement is a valid BASIC statement.

11. The asterisk will print in various positions, depending upon what BASIC system is being used. In most cases, it will print on or near print position 46.

12. The asterisk will print in various positions, depending upon what BASIC system is being used. In most cases, it will print on or near print position 30.

13. One possible program is:

10 PRINT "   *************"

There are nine blanks between the leftmost quote marks and the first asterisk.

14. One possible solution is shown on the following page.

```
 10 PRINT "              ◆                    "
 20 PRINT "          ◆      ◆                 "
 30 PRINT "       ◆             ◆             "
 40 PRINT "          ◆      ◆                 "
 50 PRINT "             ◆                     "
 60 PRINT "          ◆      ◆         ◆       "
 70 PRINT "       ◆             ◆    ◆        "
 80 PRINT "    ◆                   ◆          "
 90 PRINT "       ◆             ◆    ◆        "
100 PRINT "          ◆      ◆         ◆       "
110 PRINT "             ◆                     "
120 END
```

CHAPTER 6

1. The five arithmetic operators that you may use to cause calculations are +, -, /, *, and ↑.

2. The program will print 15, 4, and 60. The latter value was computed and assigned to D.

3. The program will print 15, 4, and 60. The value 15 × 4 is computed and printed in the PRINT statement. In Question 2, the value 15 × 4 is computed in a LET statement.

4. The program will print 5, 8, and 13. The values on the line will be approximately 15 print positions apart.

5. The program will print the values 5, 8, 40, and 0.625. All values will be printed on one line.

6. The program will print the value 40 / 10 or 4.

7. The program will print the value 60 - 3 or 57.

8. The program gives two operators in sequence. This arrangement is illegal in BASIC. The statement could be corrected to:

    60 LET C = Z ↑ (-5)

9. The BASIC statements could be these:

    10 PRINT 6 + 12/88
    20 PRINT 15/5 + 18
    30 PRINT 15/3 + 18/3
    40 END

The statement at line 30 could be:

```
30  PRINT (15 + 18) / 3
```

10. In an arithmetic expression, exponentiation is performed first.

11. Parentheses would be used in a BASIC expression in order to group values. For example, the calculation $\dfrac{A + B}{C} = ?$ must be written PRINT (A + B) / C, not A + B / C.

12. The three statements *do not* cause the same value to be computed. The first and last statements cause the same value to be printed. The middle statement gives a different answer.

13. No, extra parentheses will not harm your BASIC program in any way. When in doubt, give extra parentheses.

14. The term 4.5E4 is equivalent to the value 45000.0.

15. The term .45E-1 represents the value .045.

16. The expected result should be .41.

17. A program to give the result might be:

```
10  PRINT ((1.5E4/3.9E5) * (8.9E2/2.6E2))/9.7E4
20  END
```

18. A program to give the result might be:

```
10  PRINT ((15000/390000) * (890/260))/97000
20  END
```

CHAPTER 7

1. A BASIC function is a preprogrammed routine that is built into the BASIC programming language. To use the function, a programmer mentions it by name in a statement.

2. The function that computes square roots is SQR.

3. The names of the functions are SIN, COS, LOG and TAN.

4. The integer portion of the number 34.675 is 34.

5. The integer portion of the number 34.123 is 34.

6. The name of the function that computes integer values is INT.

7. The EXP function raises the value e (2.718281828 . . .) to some desired power.

8. The function ATN obtains the arctangent of some given tangent value.

9. The range of random numbers is from zero to 1. The value zero can arise as a random number; the value 1 cannot arise as a random number.

10. The absolute value of −81.6 is 81.6; the absolute value of 81.6 is 81.6. The name of the function that gives absolute values is ABS.

11. The *argument* of a function is the value or values that the function needs in order to give the desired result.

12. The three forms of arguments are:

   A. an actual numeric value
   B. a variable name
   C. an expression

13. A possible program is:

```
10 PRINT SQR(25)
20 END
```

14. A possible program is:

```
10 PRINT INT (-83.67)
20 END
```

15. A possible program is:

```
10 PRINT SQR (-36)
20 END
```

   The program will not give the square root of −36. It will give an error message and then give the square root of positive 36.

16. A possible program is:

```
10 PRINT ABS (-38.745)
20 END
```

17. A possible way to show that SINE divided by COSINE gives TANGENT is:

```
10 PRINT SIN (1.3) / COS (1.3)
```

```
20 PRINT TAN (1.3)
30 END
```

The two answers should be equal.

18. A possible way to show that raising a value to the $\frac{1}{2}$ power gives square root is:

```
10 PRINT 3.4 ↑ .5
20 PRINT SQR (3.4)
30 END
```

The two answers should be equal.

CHAPTER 8

1. The IF statement allows decisions to be made in a BASIC program.

2. The six relationships are:

=	equal
<	less than
>	greater than
> =	greater than or equal
< =	less than or equal
<>	not equal

3. A dummy value is used to signal the end of a series of data values. The dummy value is found with the aid of an IF statement.

4. A dummy value is some data value that is so much different from actual data values that it cannot be confused with the actual data values.

5. If the condition being tested is found to be true, the program jumps to the line number given following the words GO TO or THEN.

6. If the condition is found to be "false," the program goes to the next line in sequence.

7. The program goes to the next statement in sequence.

8. The program goes to the next statement in sequence.

9. In an IF statement, values may be:

    A. actual numbers
    B. variable names
    C. expressions

10. The words GO TO may be used in place of THEN in an IF statement.

11. One solution might be:

```
10 DATA 8.9
20 READ V
30 IF V > 5 THEN 60
40 PRINT "SMALL"
50 GO TO 70
60 PRINT "LARGE"
70 END
```

12. One solution might be:

```
10 LET A = SIN (2.6)
20 LET B = COS (1.8)
30 IF A > B THEN 60
40 PRINT "SMALL"
50 GO TO 70
60 PRINT "LARGE"
70 END
```

13. One solution is:

```
10 LET A = SIN (2.6)
20 LET B = COS (1.7)
30 LET C = LOG (8.3)
40 IF A > B GO TO 100
50 IF B > C GO TO 80
60 PRINT C
70 GO TO 130
80 PRINT B
90 GO TO 130
```

```
100  IF A > C GO TO 120
110  GO TO 60
120  PRINT A
130  END
```

14. One solution is:

```
10  DATA 2.6, 8.1, 9.7, 4.3
20  READ A, B, C, D
30  IF A < B GO TO 60
40  LET T1 = B
50  GO TO 70
60  LET T1 = A
70  IF C < D GO TO 100
80  LET T2 = D
90  GO TO 110
100  LET T2 = C
110  IF T1 < T2 GO TO 140
120  PRINT T2
130  GO TO 150
140  PRINT T1
150  END
```

15. One solution is shown below and on the next page.

```
10  DATA 2.6, 8.1, 9.7, 4.3
20  READ A, B, C, D
30  IF A < B GO TO 140
40  IF B < C GO TO 100
50  IF C < D GO TO 80
60  PRINT "FOURTH IS SMALLEST"
70  GO TO 210
80  PRINT "THIRD IS SMALLEST"
90  GO TO 210
100  IF B < D GO TO 120
110  GO TO 60
120  PRINT "SECOND IS SMALLEST"
```

```
130 GO TO 210
140 IF A < C GO TO 180
150 IF C < D GO TO 170
160 GO TO 60
170 GO TO 80
180 IF A < D GO TO 200
190 GO TO 60
200 PRINT "FIRST IS SMALLEST".
210 END
```

CHAPTER 9

1. A loop is a set of BASIC instructions that are executed more than once. Sometimes loop instructions are executed thousands of times.

2. A GO TO is useful because it causes a jump back to a part of the program that was executed earlier, thus setting up a loop.

3. The BASIC command LET is useful in setting up initial conditions. For example, a counter can be given an initial value of zero or 1.

4. The BASIC command IF can be used to test for terminating conditions.

5. A terminating condition is a situation that arises when certain variables attain certain values. For example, it may be desired to terminate a loop when the value of K is greater than 500.

6. A counter keeps track of how many times a loop is executed. For example, a variable named N might be set up to count the number of times that a loop is executed. The value 1 is added to N whenever the loop is repeated.

7. The program will give four print lines.

8. The program has an endless loop. The program keeps looping without limit. The program can be made to terminate the loop by providing a condition to be tested with an IF statement.

9. A possible program might be:

```
10 LET K = 1
20 PRINT "HOWARD KENNISON"
30 LET K = K + 1
```

```
40 IF K > 8 GO TO 60
50 GO TO 20
60 END
```

10. The program will give three print lines:

```
 5     25
10    100
15    225
```

11. A possible solution might be:

```
10 LET V = 20.6
20 PRINT V, LOG (V)
30 LET V = V + .2
40 IF V > 21.8 GO TO 60
50 GO TO 20
60 END
```

12. A possible solution might be:

```
10 LET S = 0
20 LET K = 1
30 LET S = S + K
40 LET K = K + 1
50 IF K > 20 GO TO 70
60 GO TO 30
70 PRINT S
80 END
```

CHAPTER 10

1. Statements that begin with FOR and NEXT are used in a BASIC program to simplify the construction of loops.
2. K is a counter. It will have an initial value of 1 and a final value of 35. K will increase in steps of 1.
3. The next statement needed is:

```
NEXT K
```

4. One may place as many statements between FOR and NEXT as required by the program. There may be only one statement there or several hundred.

5. STEP 7 causes the value of I to increase by 7 units each time that I is increased. The values that I takes on will be 2, 9, 16, 23, etc.

6. I will take on 143 values. They will be 2, 9, 16, 23, etc. The last value will be 996.

7. The last value that I takes on that actually will be used in the program is 992.

8. The answer to all three questions is "yes." Step sizes may be fractional values, negatives, and expressions.

9. The important value that is remembered is the value that the counter has. That is, if the FOR statement is:

    FOR K = 1 TO 200

    the value that K has will be remembered.

10. The program must return to the line that contains the NEXT statement.

11. The program will print HELLO seventeen times.

12. The program will give the following two print lines:

    9

    14

13. A possible solution might be:

    ```
    10  FOR K = 20.6 TO 21.8 STEP .2
    20  PRINT K, LOG (K)
    30  NEXT K
    40  END
    ```

14. A possible solution might be:

    ```
    10  LET A = 0
    20  LET I = (2.5 - .5)/100
    30  LET H = I/2
    40  FOR J = .5 + H TO 2.5 STEP I
    50  LET A = A + SIN(J) * I
    60  NEXT J
    ```

```
70 PRINT A
80 END
```

CHAPTER 11

1. The DIM statement sets up space for an array. For example, DIM A(20) sets up 20 locations in memory named A. The initial values in those locations are zeroes.

2. A subscript is a pointer to a particular location in an array. For example, A(3) refers to the third location of the array A.

3. The statement is:

   W(7) = 21.8

4. A loop is set up when FOR and NEXT are used. The loop can assign values directly to all locations in an array or cause those values to be read from a DATA statement.

5. The three forms of subscripts are:

   A. actual numbers
   B. variable names
   C. expressions

6. The dummy value signals the end of the data that is to be read. When the dummy value is detected with an IF statement, the program knows that there is no more data to be read.

7. The program has stored -1 in all 200 locations of the X array.

8. The program has stored the values 1, 2, 3, etc., through 200 in the 200 locations of Y.

9. The A and B arrays both contain the values 8, 7, 4, 9, 2, and 4.

10. A possible solution might be:

```
10 DATA 5, 4, 9, 8, 6
20 DIM F(5)
30 FOR K = 1 TO 5
40 READ F(K)
50 NEXT K
   .
   .
   .
   .
```

11. A possible solution might be:

```
10 DIM X(20)
20 FOR N = 1 TO 20
30 LET X(N) = 0
40 NEXT N
50 FOR K = 1 TO 20
60 PRINT X(K)
70 NEXT K
80 END
```

12. A possible solution might be:

```
10 DIM X(20)
20 FOR N = 1 TO 20
30 LET X(N) = N * 2
40 NEXT N
50 FOR K = 1 TO 20
60 PRINT X(K)
70 NEXT K
80 END
```

CHAPTER 12

1. A flowchart is a pictorial chart that shows the procedure to be used in solving some given problem.

2. A flowchart should be used for any problem requiring a computer solution especially if the procedure for solving the problem is complex.

3. When a flowchart has been created and debugged, the major portion of the planning needed to solve the problem has been completed. Writing BASIC statements to agree with the flowchart is an exceedingly simple task.

4. The oval is called the terminal symbol. It is used to represent the logical beginning and ending point of a program.

5. The parallelogram is called the I/O symbol. It is used to show where input and/or output operations are to be accomplished.

6. The only two words you might see in a parallelogram are READ and PRINT.

7. The only two words you might see in an oval are BEGIN and END (or STOP).

8. The diamond shows a point in a program where a decision is to be made.

9. The arrows leading out of a decision diamond might be labelled:

   yes   or   no
   true   or   false

   or words that mean the same. The reason that a program will take one branch or another out of a decision diamond must be clearly shown.

10. What one writes in a flowchart symbol should be easily understood by whoever reads the message.

11. The rectangle represents a calculation to be performed. For example, the calculation:

    LET D = (A + B) / C

    would be shown within a rectangle. The rectangle is called the process symbol.

12. In a flowchart, the small circle is called the connector symbol. It is used to show how one portion of a flowchart connects with another. Connectors keep flowcharts simple by avoiding long lines running here and there across the flowchart.

13. Yes, flowcharts may be oriented vertically. Some programmers prefer vertical flowcharts.

14. You can learn to flowchart by doing. At first, you should create flowcharts for all programs, even the simplest.

15. A flowchart solution might be:

16.   A possible solution might be:

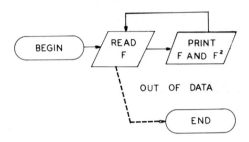

17.   A possible solution might be:

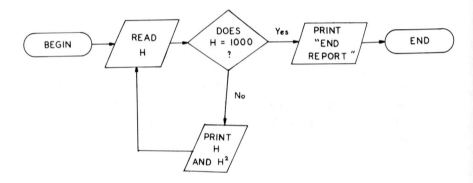

18.   A possible solution might be:

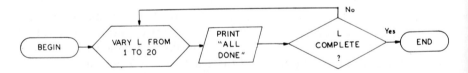

19.   A possible solution might be:

```
10  DATA 3, 8, 4, 9, 500
20  READ N
30  IF N = 500 GO TO 60
40  PRINT N, N ↑ 2
50  GO TO 20
60  PRINT "DONE"
70  END
```

20. A possible solution might be:

```
10 PRINT "SALARIES"
20 FOR K = 1 TO 300
30 READ H, R, N
40 LET P = H * R
50 PRINT H, R, P, N
60 NEXT K
70 DATA 40.5, 5.40, 135, 41.6, 5.60, 137 . . . .
80 DATA 41.5, 5.40, 138, 42.0, 6.00, 140 . . . .
            and so on . . .
999 END
```

CHAPTER 13

1. Debugging means finding the errors in a program and correcting them.

2. The timesharing system tells you that you have made one or more clerical mistakes after you type the command RUN.

3. One corrects errors in BASIC statements by retyping them. New statements replace the older ones.

4. Extra PRINT statements help debug the program by giving printouts of various critical values at various points in the program. These extra PRINT statements should be removed from the program after the program has been debugged.

5. The program has two errors:

   LEM B = 4 should be LET B = 4
   GET R = 1 should be LET R = 1

6. The program has one error. The FOR statement should read:

   FOR L = -1 TO 50 STEP 1

7. The program has one error. The DATA statement should be given ahead of the END statement.

8. The program has overlapping FOR/NEXT statements. One way to correct the program would be to give NEXT E at line 50 and NEXT D at line 60. Or, line 10 could read FOR E = and line 30 could read FOR D =.

CHAPTER 14

1. The INPUT statement allows the programmer to give input values to the program *after* the program begins to execute. When using READ, the programmer must give the data values before the program begins to execute.

2. The program prints the X values and the squares of the X values.

3. There is no limit to the number of times that the program can execute the statement at line 10. It might be only one time or it could be thousands of times.

4. The two ways to stop the program are: (1) The programmer can type STOP and return the carriage. (2) The programmer can depress the BREAK (or INTERRUPT) key.

5. The program can print a message telling what value or values are to be entered. Then the program can cause the INPUT statement to be executed.

6. An INPUT statement can give more than one variable name in its construction. Example:

    INPUT A,B,C

7. The program will execute the statements 10 times. The array A will receive 10 values.

8. The array will receive ten values.

9. A possible solution might be this:

```
10 DIM A(10)
20 FOR N = 1 TO 10
30 INPUT A(N)
40 NEXT N
```

10. A possible solution might be this:

```
10 INPUT A,B,C
20 LET S = A + B + C
30 LET Q = SQR (S)
40 PRINT A, B, C, Q
50 GO TO 10
60 END
```

CHAPTER 15

1. The ON statement allows a program to take one of several possible courses of action depending upon an ON "index."
2. You can give only two line numbers following ON or many.
3. If the ON index value is out of range, the program will print an error message and then stop.
4. If K's value is 1, the program jumps to line 30. If K's value is 2, the program jumps to line 50. If K's value is 3, the program will print an error message and then stop.
5. The program will jump to line 80 when W's value is 2 or 5.

CHAPTER 16

1. As used in BASIC, a subroutine is a set of statements that are accessed by the BASIC command GOSUB. These statements must include at least one RETURN statement.
2. The GOSUB command causes a jump to a subroutine. The program remembers where the GOSUB was so that, when RETURN is encountered in the subroutine, the program will return to the statement immediately following GOSUB.
3. In a subroutine, the RETURN statement causes a jump back to the statement immediately following the GOSUB that called the subroutine.
4. The statement at line 40 keeps the programming from accidentally falling into a subroutine. If the statement were not there, the program would go into the subroutine and cause an error message to be given when the RETURN statement was encountered.
5. Yes, a subroutine may call another subroutine.
6. Yes, a program can go into a subroutine accidentally. Refer to Question 4. If the statement at line 40 did not exist, the program would accidentally enter the subroutine area beginning at line 50.
7. The programmer should put a GO TO statement just ahead of the subroutine area. Refer to Question 4. The GO TO statement at line 40 keeps the programmer from falling accidentally into the subroutine area.
8. The program will add A and B when A's value is less than B's value. The program will multiply C's value by D's value when

C's value is greater than D's value. To eliminate two RETURNs from this program, line 120 could be changed to GO TO 140, and line 220 could be changed to GO TO 240.

The program contains two subroutines. There is a GO TO at line 60 to keep the program from accidentally falling into the first subroutine.

The value E does not need be initialized at the program's beginning because both subroutines always give it a value of some kind at some point within the subroutines.

9. The remark line in a BASIC program gives a documentation comment about the program. The remark helps others understand what the program does.

10. The word remark might be spelled REM, REMARK, REMBRANDT, or many other ways as long as the first three letters of the word are REM.

11. The program doesn't print anything. All lines except the last are remarks.

12. Definitely yes. Many complex programs could not be understood unless the programmer had been thoughtful enough to include many remarks in the program.

CHAPTER 17

1. The statement could be:

    ```
    200 LET Q$ = "TRUMBULL"
    ```

2. The program will print:

    ```
    THE DATAIS CORRECT
    ```

    There is no blank between the words DATA and IS.

3. An alphanumeric name follows the same rules as a numeric name except that a dollar sign is added to the name. Examples:

    ```
    X$, W$, M6$
    ```

4. Yes, alphanumeric values can be read from a DATA statement. Example:

```
10 DATA AIRLINE
20 READ D$
```

5. Yes, alphanumeric values can be obtained with an INPUT statement. Example:

```
10 INPUT F$
```

Quotes would be given around the value being obtained if the value

    a. contained one or more blanks
    b. contained digits or hyphens
    c. contained one or more commas

It is not incorrect to always give quotes around values being entered via INPUT.

6. A possible solution might be:

```
10 LET N$ = "THOMAS WORTH"
20 FOR K = 1 TO 5
30 PRINT N$
40 NEXT K
50 END
```

CHAPTER 18

1. Random numbers are numbers given by the computer. They are completely unpredictable. That is, a program that requires a random number does not know ahead of time what that number is. Random numbers are used to simulate occurrences in everyday life or to allow computer games.

2. The largest random number that BASIC gives is a number that is just a tiny bit smaller than 1. The smallest random number is zero. The range of random numbers, therefore, is from zero to 1 where zero is a possibility but 1 is not.

3. The name of the built-in routine is RND.

4. The three types of arguments that may be given to the RND function are shown on the next page.

0   This gives a set of random numbers that is always the
        same. In a sense, it's a standard set of random num-
        bers that can be used while debugging a program.

-1   (Or any negative number) This gives an unpredictable
        and unrepeatable set of random numbers. Every time
        the program is run, a different set of random num-
        bers is given.

1   (Or any positive number greater than zero) This gives an
        unpredictable random number sequence. However,
        it is repeatable. If one gives the number 89 or 7.5 or
        137 as an argument, the same set of random numbers
        will be given every time that argument is used.

5. The average of a set of random numbers would most likely be
   .5. The average might not be *exactly* .5 but a value very close
   to it.

6. The equation needed is:

   N = INT (RND (A) * M) + B

   where N is the desired number; A is the argument of the random number function; M is the number of numbers in the
   desired series of numbers; and B is the beginning number of
   the series. For example, if a random number were desired in
   the series 8, 9, 10, 11, 12, the formula could be:

   N = INT (RND (-1) * 5 + 8

7. The number is unknown. It lies somewhere between zero
   and 1. Zero is possible but 1 is not.

8. It's impossible to determine whether the program will print
   A, B, or C. The random number given cannot be predicted.

9. The computer will print the number 4. The value .237457
   multiplied by 5 and converted to an integer is 1. When 3 is
   added, the value assigned to H becomes 4.

10. It is possible for D's value to be zero. It is not possible for
    D's value to be 1.

CHAPTER 19

1. A two-dimensional array is an area in memory that is arranged in the form of rows and columns. When numbers are

read into that area, the area becomes a matrix.   An array, therefore, represents *space* arranged in rows and columns. A matrix arises when numbers are loaded into the array.

2. The array looks like this:

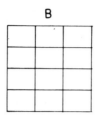

B

3. The DIM statement could be:

   10 DIM R(5,6)

4. The matrix looks like this:

H

9	4	5
6	8	3

5. The matrix looks like this:

H

9	5	8
4	6	3

6. The matrix looks like this:

H

9	4	5
6	8	3

7. The matrix looks like this internally:

$\bar{C}$

3	8	0	0
9	4	0	0
7	6	0	-0
0	0	0	0

But the PRINT command at line 40 causes this printout:

C

3	8
9	4
7	6

8. The program will not operate properly because there should be 20 values in the DATA statement but there are only 16. There will be an OUT OF DATA message.

9. MAT READ obtains values from the DATA statement. MAT INPUT obtains values entered by a programmer *after* the program has begun to execute.

10. The output would be:

7

4

9

3

2

11. The program could be:

```
010 DIM T (5,5)
020 FOR K = 1 TO 5
030 FOR L = 1 TO 5
040 LET T(K,L) = 0
050 NEXT L
```

```
060 NEXT K
070 FOR N = 1 TO 5
080 LET T(N,N) = 1
090 NEXT N
100 MAT PRINT T
110 END
```

Note: See the description of the zero identity matrices in this chapter.

12. A possible solution might be:

```
100 DIM W(5,5)
110 FOR  J = 1 TO 5
120 FOR  K = 1 TO 5
130 LET W(J,K) = 1
140 NEXT K
150 NEXT J
160 FOR  L = 2 TO 4
170 FOR  M = 2 TO 4
180 LET W(L,M) = 0
190 NEXT M
200 NEXT L
210 MAT PRINT W
220 END
```

Note: See the description of the constant 1 matrix in this chapter.

13. Every element in two matrices is summed, and the result is placed in the same relative position of a third matrix. That is, $A(1,1)$ is added to $B(1,1)$ and the result is placed in $C(1,1)$, etc.

14. The C matrix will look like this:

C

-3	3	1
-5	7	8
-1	-2	5

15. Yes. This text does not go into an explanation of that term.

16. Inversion of matrices is used to find roots.

17. The matrix would look like this:

4	4	6
8	6	8
3	9	3

18. The matrix would look like this:

D

21	27	18
18	15	9
12	0	24

19. The matrix would look like this:

F

1	1	1	1
1	1	1	1
1	1	1	1
1	1	1	1

20. The matrix would look like this:

F

0	0	0	0
0	0	0	0
0	0	0	0
0	0	0	0

21. The matrix would look like this:

F

1	0	0	0
0	1	0	0
0	0	1	0
0	0	0	1

22. The five matrix types are:

MAT READ
MAT INPUT
CON
ZER
IDN

23. A possible solution might be:

```
100 DATA 17, 24, 1, 8, 15, 23, 5, 7, 14, 16
110 DATA 4, 6, 13, 20, 22, 10, 12, 19, 21
120 DATA 3, 11, 18, 25, 2, 9
130 DIM D (5,5)
140 MAT READ D
150 MAT PRINT D
160 END
```

24. A possible solution might be:

```
100 DATA A, B, C, D, E, F, G, H, J, K, L
110 DATA M, N, O, P, Q, R, S, T, U, V, W
120 DATA X, Y, Z
130 DIM A$ (5,5)
140 MAT READ A$
150 MAT PRINT A$
160 END
```

CHAPTER 20

1. The PRINT SPC command gives blanks on a print line. For example:

    PRINT SPC(5); "*"

    gives five blanks ahead of an asterisk on a print line.

2. The equals sign will print in print position 18.

3. The three forms of arguments for the PRINT SPC command are:

    A. an actual numeric value
    B. a variable name
    C. an expression

4. The program will give this output:

    1

    2

    3

    There are three blanks ahead of the values 1, 2, and 3.

5. The PRINT TAB command causes tabbing to desired print positions.

6. The PRINT TAB command may use three types of arguments. They are:

    A. an actual numeric value
    B. a variable name
    C. an expression

7. The output will look like this:

    1

    2

    3

    The values 1, 2, and 3 print in print position 5 because of the PRINT TAB(5) command.

8. The values of B and $B \uparrow 2$ will begin at print positions 10 and 20.

9. A possible solution might be:

```
100 DATA 18, 10, 3, 7, 16, 31, 46, 43, 49, 47
120 FOR K = 1 TO 10
130 READ X
140 PRINT TAB (X + .5); "*"
150 NEXT K
160 END
```

10. A possible solution might be:

```
100 DATA 36, 51, 73, 105, 90, 85, 100
110 DATA 120, 135, 124
120 FOR K = 1 TO 10
130 READ X
140 LET P = ((X - 36)/(135 - 36) * 70) + .5
150 PRINT TAB (P); "*"
160 NEXT K
170 END
```

11. A possible solution might be:

```
100 PRINT     "                    ◆                    "
110 PRINT     "               ◆         ◆               "
120 PRINT     "          ◆         ◆         ◆          "
130 PRINT     "     ◆         ◆    ◆    ◆         ◆     "
140 PRINT     "          ◆         ◆         ◆          "
150 PRINT     "               ◆         ◆               "
160 PRINT     "                    ◆                    "
170 END
```

12. A possible solution might be:

```
100 PRINT     "◆  ◆  ◆  ◆  ◆  ◆"
110 PRINT     "◆  ◆  ◆  ◆  ◆  ◆"
120 PRINT     "◆  ◆  ◆            "
130 PRINT     "◆  ◆  ◆  ◆  ◆  ◆"
140 PRINT     "            ◆  ◆  ◆"
150 PRINT     "◆  ◆  ◆  ◆  ◆  ◆"
160 PRINT     "◆  ◆  ◆  ◆  ◆  ◆"
170 END
```

CHAPTER 21

1. PRINT USING allows the precise positioning of values in an output line.

2. The program prints the value of A beginning at print position 5 of the output paper. A's value will be given rounded to 2 decimal places. Note that there are four blanks between the colon and the first pound sign (#) on line 30.

3. The PRINT USING format line (line 80) shows only one print image—the one associated with A's value. There should be another print image associated with B's value.

4. E's value will print beginning at print position 4. Note that there are three blanks between the colon and the first pound sign (#) on line 110.

5. The program will print $25.85. The dollar sign ($) will print in print position 11. Note that there are 10 blanks between the colon and the dollar sign ($) on line 120.

6. The program will print COST REPORT beginning at print position 6. Note that there are five blanks between the colon and the letter C on line 300.

7. Up arrows (↑) are used when the value to be printed employs powers of 10. The value of F might appear as 3.78E 10.

8. The computer will print −38.47. The negative sign will print in print position 6.

9. An alphabetic or alphanumeric item might need to be printed adjusted left. If the value JONES needs to be printed, it will be adjusted to the left in the print image 'LLLLLLL. The letter J will print in print position 1.

10. An alphabetic or alphanumeric item might need to be printed adjusted right. If the value BEN needs to be printed, it will be adjusted to the right in the print image 'RRRRR.

11. An alphabetic or alphanumeric item might need to be printed centered in the print image 'CCCCCCCCC.

12. The computer will print ****. The value 305.6 needs a print image having five character positions. The image ##.# contains only four.

CHAPTER 22

1. A file is an organized collection of data values concerning some definite subject.

2. To read a file means to obtain some data from the file.

3. The command checks file #1 to determine whether there is more data that can be read from file #1. The check is made before an attempt is made to read the file. If there is no data in the file, the READ command is bypassed.

4. The data are being read from file #2. This file is Y-FILE.

5. The data values in the file should have commas separating them. The lines should read:

    10 8.6, 3.5, 4.2,
    20 9.7, 1.2, 7.5,
    30 8.5, 9.6, 9.8,
    40 7.6, 8.1, 1.3,

    Note that there are no commas following line numbers 10, 20, 30, 40.

6. A valid name for the file might be IN-DATA. Other acceptable names are X, IN-FILE, VALUES, etc. The name of a file may consist of up to eight alphabetic characters.

7. The SCRATCH command changes a file input/output made from the standard READ to WRITE. That is, a program will not allow you to write into a file unless the file has been SCRATCHd, i.e., changed to write mode.

8. A file may be either read from or written into. All created files are initially in READ mode. If you want to write into the same file, you must change the file's mode from READ to WRITE. You can do this with the SCRATCH command.

9. The program will write in file 3. The WRITE command leads off each line in the file with a line number. The PRINT command will write lines into the file without leading line numbers.

10. A file can be read by changing the file's mode from WRITE to READ. The mode can be changed with the use of the RESTORE command. For example, RESTORE #1 will change file 1's mode from WRITE to READ.

11. The command BACKSPACE backspaces a file. To backspace one data value, the BACKSPACE command could be given this way:

    BACKSPACE #2

12. The RESTORE command changes a file's mode from WRITE to READ.

13. A possible solution to the problem might be:

```
100 FILES INPUT3; OUTPUT4
110 SCRATCH #2
120 IF END #1 THEN 160
130 READ #1, A, B, C, D
140 WRITE #2, A, B, C, D
150 GO TO 120
160 END
```

14. The errors are:

Line 10   A semicolon must separate file names, not a comma.

Line 20   The wrong file is being scratched. It should be #2.

Line 30   THEN GO TO is incorrect. The phrase should be either THEN or GO TO, but not both THEN and GO TO.

Line 40   A comma should separate data values, not a semicolon.

Line 60   The program goes to the wrong place. It should go to Line 30.

Line 70   This command is incorrect. The program must not go to Line 30 after the input file has been completely processed. The program should print "END OF RUN." The line at statement 30 should read IF END #1 THEN 80.

CHAPTER 23

1. The nine functions are:

SIN

COS

TAN

SQR

ABS

LOG

INT

EXP

RND

2. A "home-made" function is a function that a programmer may invent for his or her program. The function can be either a one-line definition or a multiple-line function. The victim record is stored in from one to many records. For example, if JOE TIMMIS' record is to be stored in memory it would require seven character pages for storage in C.

3. The three forms of arguments may be:

    A. actual number
    B. a variable that represents a value
    C. an expression

4. The three characters are DEF.

5. A created function may employ more than one line.

6. A possible solution might be:

    100 DEF WCC (W) = (W + 9.6)/W ↑ 2

7. A possible solution might be:

    100 DEF BCC (B,C) = (B + C)/(B + 5.8)

8. The variables are dummies because they are stand-ins for actual values that will be supplied by the program. Dummy names are replaced with numeric values, *other* variable names, and/or expressions.

9. The function definition does not show Y's value being used.

10. The function definition does not show A as one of the variables used in the execution of the function. In other words, the function requires two values in order to function as expected. One variable representing those values is A and another is B. The function definition should be:

    DEF JOE (A,B) = (A + B) / (A - 5.8)

11. The program will print 1.33333 as R's value.

12. The program will print 12 as Z's value.

CHAPTER 24

1. A string is a series of characters made up of letters of the alphabet, digits, and special characters.

2. The two actions that CHANGE might perform are:

    a. convert the characters in a string to a series of numeric codes with one code for each character in the string.

    b. convert a series of numeric codes to a string.

3. A DIM statement is needed because the numeric codes that the string involves must be stored in an array. The DIM statement gives the size and name of the array. Location zero of the array gives the size of the string, that is, its length in characters.

4. The two-digit numeric codes for the word TYPE are:

    84 (T)
    89 (Y)
    80 (P)
    69 (E)

5. The statement converts the characters in the string D$ to numeric values in the array H. If the D$ string contains the word DATA, the array H will contain the values 05, 68, 65, 84, and 65.

6. The statement changes the array T to the numeric string A$. If the array contains the values 07, 84, 89, 80, 69, 32, 73, 78, the string will consist of the characters TYPE IN.

7. Yes, H must be an array.

8. Yes, T must be an array.

9. The program will print TEST.

10. A possible solution to the problem might be:

```
100 DIM H(26), P(2)
110 LET H (0) = 26
120 LET V = 65
130 FOR J = 1 TO 26
140 LET H(J) = V
150 LET V = V + 1
160 NEXT J
```

```
170 FOR K = 1 TO 26
180 LET P(0) = 2
190 LET P(1) = H(K)
200 LET P(2) = 32
210 CHANGE P TO B$
220 PRINT H(K), B$
230 NEXT K
240 END
```

The entry at line 110 is not necessary. It is included merely for program documentation.

GLOSSARY

Absolute Value: The positive form of any given number. Thus, the absolute value of 187 is 187, and the absolute value of -96 is 96.

Array: A set of values arranged in a regular pattern such as in single-file or in two dimensions.

Assignment Statement: A BASIC statement that begins with the word LET. The value that is shown on the right hand side of the equal sign is stored in the name given on the left hand side.

BASIC: A computer programming language that is useful for scientific and business problem solving.

BASIC Statement: *See* Statement.

Body of Statement: The main part of a BASIC statement; the part that immediately follows the key word.

Break Key: A key on the keyboard of a terminal that may be used to stop a program which appears to be in a loop.

Cell: *See* Memory Cell.

Computer: An electronic device used for making calculations and for processing business data. Two of a computer's most impressive characteristics are extremely high processing speeds and very large memory capacities.

Conditional Statement: A statement that requires a test to be made. An IF statement is a conditional statement since the computer will take one of two alternate paths.

Conversational Timesharing: *See* Timesharing.

Cosine: In a right triangle, the value obtained when the side adjacent to an angle is divided by the hypotenuse.

Data: The input values that a computer must have in order to solve a given problem.

Data Name: A BASIC name having one or two characters to which a value can be assigned.

Decrement: To decrease the value of a counter.

Dimension: The number of elements in an array and their configuration (one or two dimensions). In BASIC, the DIM statement gives the dimensions of an array.

Disk: *See* Magnetic Disk.

e: A never-ending number used in mathematics. The first few digits of the number are 2.718281828.

Exponentiation: Raising a value to some power. Thus,

$$100 \ \ LET \ R = W \uparrow 5$$

is the same as

$$100 \ \ LET \ R = W * W * W * W * W$$

Expression: In an assignment statement, the value to the right of the equal sign.

File: A collection of data to be used with a computer program. The program itself is often called a file.

Flowchart: A pictorial representation of what you want the computer to do and in what sequence.

Flowcharting: The process of developing a flowchart.

ID: Your personal identification validating your right to use a distant computer in timesharing mode.

Increment: To increase the value of a counter.

Information: The output given by a computer program. The answers to the problem.

Initialization: Giving first values to a data name. In loops, counters are normally initialized to 1.

Input: The values that a program must have in order to solve a given problem (*see also* Data).

Integer: A whole number.

Key Word: In BASIC, the first word of a statement that identifies the type of statement. Some key words are LET, IF, GO TO, PRINT, etc.

Line Number: An identifying number that is placed ahead of each BASIC statement in a program.

Log (Base 10): The value to which 10 must be raised in order to obtain a given value. (The base 10 log of 100 is 2.)

Log (Natural): The value to which "e" must be raised in order to obtain a given value. (The natural log of 1 is 0.)

Log-on Procedure: The questions and answers between a distant computer and the user that validate the user and permit him to begin using the computer.

Loop: A set of statements that are executed over and over.

Magnetic Disk: Computer hardware upon which programs and/or data files may be stored.

Matrix: An arrangement of related values either in one or two dimensions.

Memory: A computer can store electronically within its mechanism several million characters of information at any given moment. In back up devices, computers can store several trillion characters for relatively immediate use.

Memory Cell: A unit in the memory of a computer capable of holding one or more characters of data. A memory cell can also hold numeric values.

Output: The answers given by a computer program (*see also* Information).

Permanent Storage Space: A place in a computer system, usually a magnetic disk, where programs can be stored for a given length of time.

Print: To print answers on the output paper available with your terminal.

Processing Speed: A computer can do as much computing, and other data processing, in one second as a person can do in one year.

Program: A set of instructions telling a computer how to solve a given problem. The instructions are given in a programming language such as BASIC.

Programmer: A person who develops computer programs.

Programming: The process of developing a computer program.

Read: To obtain data from a DATA statement.

Relational Symbols: The symbols $>$, $=$, and $<$ that may be used to indicate whether one value is larger, smaller, equal, or not equal to another. Relational symbols are used in IF statements.

Return Key: A key on a terminal's keyboard that is used to enter a BASIC statement that has been typed.

Search: The finding of a particular value in a table or array.

Sentinel Value: A value found in a DATA statement that signals the end of the data values.

Sine: In a right triangle, the value obtained when the side opposite the angle is divided by the hypotenuse.

Square Root: The number which, when multiplied by itself, gives a given number. Thus, the square root of 64 is 8.

Statement: A single instruction to the computer such as

$$10 \ \ \text{LET P} = 42.6$$

Step Size: The value by which a counter of a loop is changed.

Subscript: A number, name, or expression that tells which one of an array element is to be worked with.

System Command: A command directly to the computer telling it to do something with a program you have created or wish to create. Some system commands are SAVE, UNSAVE, LIST, RUN, NEW, OLD. BYE is also a system command that disconnects you from the distant computer.

Table: *See* Array.

Tangent: In a right triangle, the value obtained when the side opposite the angle is divided by the side adjacent to the angle.

Terminal: A device that looks like a teletype or a typewriter on a large stand. Through it a user can gain access to a distant computer and converse with the computer to solve a given problem.

Test: To check out, such as the value of a counter, the state of a condition, a program, etc.

Timesharing: A method of using a computer by means of the telephone. This system allows many people to be connected to the distant computer at the same time. The computer shares its time among all users.

Variable Name: *See* Data Name.

Working Area: A place in the computer's memory where you can work with arrays.

Working Space: A place in a computer where you can work with programs.

Zone: One of the five areas on the terminal output paper where an answer may be printed.

INDEX